PSALM 23

*The Lord is my shepherd; I shall not want.*

*He maketh me to lie down in green pastures; he leadeth me beside the still waters.*

*He restoreth my soul; he leadeth me in the paths of righteousness for his name's sake.*

*Yea, though I walk through the valley of the shadow of death, I will fear no evil; for thou art with me; thy rod and thy staff they comfort me.*

*Thou preparest a table before me in the presence of mine enemies; thou anointest my head with oil; my cup runneth over.*

*Surely goodness and mercy shall follow me all the days of my life; and I will dwell in the house of the Lord for ever.*

# GOODNESS, YOU'RE FOLLOWING ME!

A Devotional Commentary on Psalm 23

By Bill Popejoy

Gospel Publishing House
Springfield, Missouri
02-0519

*I dedicate this book to Doris, who became my bride on November 27, 1947, and who has been my faithful companion on the journey toward eternal life.*

© 1975 by Bill Popejoy. Copyright assigned to Gospel Publishing House, Springfield, Missouri 65802. All rights reserved. No part of the text may be reproduced in any form without written permission of the publishers, except brief quotations used in connection with reviews in magazines or newspapers. Printed in the United States of America. ISBN 0-88243-519-1

# CONTENTS

# PSALM
## TWENTY-THREE

The twenty-third Psalm is the most well-known chapter of the Bible. More people can quote this—the Shepherd Psalm—than any other complete chapter of Scripture. Boys and girls in Sunday School earn a star on a chart for memorizing it. Preachers quote it at gravesides. And bookmarks call constant attention to it.

Yet, I wonder, do we know this transcendent Psalm at all? Have we even begun to enter into the revelation of its riches? Are we so awed by its beauty that we hesitate to actually touch it? Have we stood barefoot, on holy ground, mesmerized by the fascinating fire, without hearing the Voice that ordains to service?

There is a parallel in the New Testament scene. John, the beloved apostle, wrote of Jesus, "And the Word was made flesh, and dwelt among us, (and we beheld his glory, the glory as of the only begotten of the Father,) full of grace and truth" (John 1:14). On the mount of transfiguration John beheld the glory of the Lord. He saw Jesus transformed before his very eyes, and the sight was too much for him. We are not yet equipped to look upon the glory of the Lord; that day will come when we are "clothed upon with our house which is from heaven" (II Corinthians 5:2).

But John wrote something else: "That which was from the beginning, which we have heard, which we have seen with our eyes, which we have looked upon, and our hands have handled, of the Word of life" (I John 1:1). There you have it—"our hands have handled"!

It is one thing to behold the glory, and quite another to handle the Word of life! To do nothing but view the wonder will result in a lethargic "deep sleep." To do nothing but handle the Word will result in critical irreverence. There must be a proper balance between beholding and handling.

Yet we have held the twenty-third Psalm only as something to be wondered at as on a mount of transfiguration! We have come very near to idolizing it—keeping it in a safe place, far removed from day-by-day living. It has been a little "god" on a pedestal, and we dared not touch it. We have walked on tiptoe in its presence, as though it were a china doll which might fall over and break!

Take it, and examine it closely! You won't hurt it. God didn't put that chapter in your Bible as an untouchable shrine, only to be adored from a distance. It is to be a lamp unto your feet, and a light unto your path (Psalm 119:105). "All scripture is given by inspiration of God, and is profitable for doctrine, for reproof, for correction, for instruction in righteousness: That the man of God may be perfect, thoroughly furnished unto all good works" (II Timothy 3:16, 17). And the Shepherd Psalm is Scripture!

It is a psalm. It was written to be sung. It is to be part of living. It contains messages of comfort, discipline, restoration, revelation, direction, provision, relevance, anointing, blessing, and hope. It embraces the entirety of living for God. It deals with our Lord's methods of administering "goodness and mercy" both during "the days of my life" and "forever."

The twenty-third Psalm beautifully portrays our heavenly Father's care and concern for us. What is a sheep worth? Yet God gave His Son to die for even one straying lamb! Oh, what wondrous love! Maybe this is one of our reasons for neglecting to diligently search out these inspired words—the light of divine love dazzles us! But let us attempt to look anyhow.

Have you noticed the slow and undefinable transition in the Psalm? At the outset "The Lord is my shepherd" and I am His sheep. In a moment, however, I am seated at a table in the Lord's house—that is not the position of a sheep but of a son!

You see, the Shepherd-sheep relationship is a parable. The Father-son relationship is a fact. We need to understand this clearly: we do not graduate from sheep to sons. This is not an either/or relationship. One is simply a picture; the other is a reality.

Dr. C. I. Scofield calls our attention to the

position of this Psalm. In his notes he writes, "Psalms 22., 23., and 24. form a trilogy. In Psalm 22. the *good* Shepherd gives His life for the sheep (John 10. 11); in Psalm 23. the *great* Shepherd, 'brought again from the dead through the blood of the everlasting covenant' (Heb. 13. 20), tenderly cares for the sheep; in Psalm 24. the *chief* Shepherd appears as King of glory to own and reward the sheep (I Pet. 5. 4)."

The twenty-second Psalm is history. The twenty-fourth Psalm is prophecy. But the twenty-third Psalm is now. If you are looking for something meaningful and relevant, here it is. In inspired poetic language, God speaks to us today.

We will not argue with the critics about either the identity of the human penman of these words or about the exact date of writing. For our part, we accept David as the writer. And we simply do not know whether he wrote this while watching sheep as a young man or while as an old man remembering watching sheep. We leave such bickering to those who have nothing better to do.

Whoever pushed the pencil, the Holy Spirit wrote these words. And reverently we approach them, knowing that we are walking on holy ground. We pray earnestly for divine direction as we read:

"The Lord is my shepherd; I shall not want. He maketh me to lie down in green pastures: he leadeth me beside the still waters. He restoreth my soul: he leadeth me in the paths of righteousness for his name's sake. Yea, though I walk through the valley of the shadow of death, I will fear no evil: for thou art with me; thy rod and thy staff they comfort me. Thou preparest a table before me in the presence of mine enemies: thou anointest my head with oil; my cup runneth over. Surely goodness and mercy shall follow me all the days of my life: and I will dwell in the house of the Lord for ever."

# SHEEP, OR SONS?

Under divine inspiration the ancient psalmist wrote, "The Lord is my shepherd" (Psalm 23:1).

With equal anointing the New Testament apostle penned, "Ye have received the Spirit of adoption, whereby we cry, Abba, Father" (Romans 8:15).

Which one was correct? Am I a sheep or a son? Is God my Shepherd or my Father? Was I bought or born? Do I live in a meadow or a house? Am I chattel or family?

These are relevant questions. I cannot have any meaningful relationship with the Almighty God until I can identify that relationship. There must be no ambiguity. Abstract associations are meaningless. When I approach Him, when I think of Him, when I speak of Him, my mind must be clear about a few things. I must not only believe that He exists but that there is a vital relationship between us. And I must know what that relationship is.

The problem would be solved if the twenty-third Psalm were the only scriptural reference to a Shepherd-sheep relationship. Then we could say that in Old Testament times God's people were sheep, but under the new covenant "now are we the sons of God" (I John 3:2).

But the tenth chapter of John's Gospel contains one of the most transcendent discourses of our Lord—in which He identifies Himself as the Good Shepherd! Beautifully mixing His metaphors, Jesus speaks of people as sheep. Note, for example, verse nine: "I am the door: by me if any man enter in, he shall be saved, and shall go in and out, and find pasture." Men have no need for pastures; sheep do.

As a matter of fact, I can neither appreciate nor fulfill my position as a son of God until I happily rejoice in my position as one of His sheep. As a sheep I follow. As a son I inherit. And I will not inherit unless I follow!

Our regal position in the family of God is being stressed a great deal nowadays. We are told about our "rights and privileges" as sons. We are admonished to enter boldly into the presence of our Father. We hear about sitting on thrones and treading on serpents. The emphasis is that we should rise to our full stature in Christ. Body ministry is the theme of the day. Our goal is to be the "perfect man," lacking nothing (Ephesians 4:13). And all our conflicts must be won through our might in Christ.

Now these truths are not to be ignored. We *are* children of God. The family relationship in the body of Christ is fundamental to victorious living. As sons we are heirs of all the promises of God. As sons, "His royal blood now flows through our veins."

However, we must beware lest we separate sons

from sheep. In the divine economy they are one. Here is the proof: Jesus said, "I am the good shepherd: the good shepherd giveth his life for the sheep" (John 10:11). Now, no one ever lays down his life for a mere sheep—not willingly. Sheep simply aren't worth it. But a father would lay down his life for his son.

No other picture can so adequately portray our dependence upon God as the simple yet powerful statement, "The Lord is my shepherd." Note, *my* position is not even stated, and I must not read something into it which is not intended. It is so very easy to read, "The Lord is my shepherd," while thinking, "I am one of the Lord's sheep."

While the latter is true, it commits a basic error in Christian philosophy: it shifts attention from the Shepherd to the sheep. The statement is not about *me*—although I am involved in it; the statement is about my *Shepherd*. I must never brag about being one of the Master's sheep, but I will boast both now and in eternity that Jesus is my Shepherd.

This shift of attention is the very basis of the picture in this great Psalm. Read it again, and you will see what I mean. *His* ownership, *His* provision, *His* direction, *His* care and concern—these constitute the theme.

For, you see, the sheep is not a loner. These animals require more attention and more care than any other class of livestock. Leave them "on their own," and they will die or be killed. Their survival is totally dependent on their owner.

This is terribly humbling to the human "ego." And for this reason we prefer to talk about being sons of God. To be a sheep is so degrading! It means you're not even smart enough to survive. It means you live only by the mob instinct. It means that fears and timidity, stubbornness and stupidity, low and perverse habits are your only moral assets!

But that's the way we are! If we survive, all praise goes to the Shepherd! The Lord is not fortunate to have me as one of His sheep. But I am mighty fortunate to have Him as my Shepherd!

Read again the tenth chapter of the Gospel of John, and see how much our Shepherd cares for His sheep. He loves them and protects them. He speaks to them and leads them. He gives them eternal life.

Sheep are nearsighted. They do not even see well enough to recognize their shepherd. But they recognize his *voice*. That is enough. They will not worry about danger over the next hilltop. Their only concern is to stay near enough to the shepherd to hear his voice. Their total confidence is in Him. He will defend them. So long as they can hear him they have no cause for concern. "The sheep follow him: for they know his voice" (John 10:4).

Stay near Jesus! Stop exploring every nearby bush. Don't toy with the idea of your own brilliance or strength. Depend on it: as a sheep you can neither fight and win, nor run fast enough to escape.

Lie flat on your face in total recognition of your weakness, and say, "The Lord is my shepherd."

# I
# WILL BE
# CONTENT

"I shall not want," sang the shepherd-psalmist. Did David pen these lines? If he did, the meaning comes into a more profound focus. For David knew what it was to live in caves, to be hunted and hungry. He experienced the horrors of loneliness and exile, away from family and friends. Yet he wrote, "I shall not want!"

(Whether he wrote as a young man tending his father's sheep or as a king recalling God's blessings is irrelevant; the message remains the same. If these lines were merely one man's experience, they would be interesting but meaningless. They were, however, "given by inspiration of God," and are "profitable for doctrine, for reproof, for correction, for instruction in righteousness" [II Timothy 3:16].)

"I shall not want." The phrase itself has two meanings. It may be interpreted, "I shall not have any lack or need." Or it may simply mean, "I will be content with what I have."

The first interpretation is impossible. To insinuate that God's people never have real needs is absurd. The pages of Scripture are replete with descriptions of great men and women of God who experienced severe personal privation and adversity.

There is quite a gospel of prosperity which is sweeping across our land today. It proudly proclaims that material blessings may be equated with godliness: if a Christian prospers in the things of this world, he is distinguished as a man of superior faith!

All this, however, goes smack in the face of the warning of Revelation 3:17, "Because thou sayest, I am rich and increased with goods, and have need of nothing; and knowest not that thou art wretched, and miserable, and poor, and blind, and naked."

A rich young ruler came to Jesus, wanting to be His disciple. Any church would be proud to have a member like that! But our Lord "beholding him loved him, and said unto him, One thing thou lackest: go thy way, sell whatsoever thou hast, and give to the poor, and thou shalt have treasure in heaven: and come, take up the cross and follow me" (Mark 10:21).

Think about it. Jesus said to a man who had everything, "One thing thou lackest!" Then human need cannot be measured by *things*. "For a man's life consisteth not in the abundance of the things which he possesseth" (Luke 12:15).

Since Scripture must be interpreted in the light of Scripture, and since the disciple's commission is to "rightly divide the word of truth" (II Timothy 2:15), we must accept the psalmist's affirmation, "I shall not want," as meaning, "I will be content."

Worry is one of the deadliest enemies of the Christian life. It saps away all strength. It nullifies

17

apparent victories. It neutralizes faith, making it ineffective.

Worry is discontent. It is unhappiness with circumstances as they are, and is really more interested in changing environments than in changing the environment! Worry walks the floor and gets ulcers. Worry never thanks God for things as they are and is miserable.

In His sermon on the mount, our Lord gave explicit instructions to His followers on this subject—instructions which have the obvious goal of a life of contentment in Christ. He said, "Therefore I say unto you, Take no thought for your life, what ye shall eat or what ye shall drink; nor yet for your body, what ye shall put on. Is not the life more than meat, and the body than raiment? Behold the fowls of the air: for they sow not, neither do they reap, nor gather into barns; yet your heavenly Father feedeth them. Are ye not much better than they? Which of you by taking thought can add one cubit unto his stature? And why take ye thought for raiment? Consider the lilies of the field, how they grow; they toil not, neither do they spin: And yet I say unto you, that even Solomon in all his glory was not arrayed like one of these. Wherefore if God so clothe the grass of the field, which today is, and tomorrow is cast into the oven, shall he not much more clothe you, O ye of little faith? Therefore, take no thought, saying, What shall we eat? or, What shall we drink? or, Wherewithal shall we be clothed? (For after all these things do the

Gentiles seek:) for your heavenly Father knoweth that ye have need of all these things. But seek ye first the kingdom of God and his righteousness; and all these things shall be added unto you" (Matthew 6:25-33).

Live like Jesus told you to live, sir, and you will be free from worry. You will relax in God, and say, "The Lord is my shepherd; I shall not worry."

The apostle Paul learned and demonstrated this victorious trust in Jesus. From Rome's dungeon he wrote to the Philippian Christians, "I have learned, in whatsoever state I am, therewith to be content. For I know how to be abased, and I know how to abound; every where and in all things I am instructed both to be full and to be hungry, both to abound and to suffer need. I can do all things through Christ which strengtheneth me" (Philippians 4:11-13).

The same apostle who wrote, "Even unto this present hour we both hunger, and thirst, and are naked, and are buffeted, and have no certain dwelling place; and labor, working with our own hands: being reviled, we bless; being persecuted, we suffer it; being defamed we entreat: we are made as the filth of the world, and are the offscouring of all things unto this day" (I Corinthians 4:11-13), also wrote, "But I have all, and abound" (Philippians 4:18).

The secret of Paul's tremendously victorious life for God was in his genuine satisfaction with circumstances. He accepted whatever happened as part of the itinerary which his Lord had outlined for him on this planet. His happiness was no facade. He thanked God for everything. He was content.

Out of discontentment grows envy, strife, bitterness, hatred, malice, and jealousy. Be content, and these evil tendencies cannot raise their ugly heads. In Christ, you do not live "under the circumstances"; you live *above* them!

The sheep does not worry about tomorrow's pasture, or about a weather report, or about the possibility of rustlers stealing some lambs. He leaves all such things in the hands of his shepherd.

Let us go to the sheep and learn to say, "The Lord is my shepherd; I shall not want."

# LIE
# DOWN!

"He maketh me to lie down in green pastures." The picture is of a shepherd and his sheep. And it is a type of one aspect of our relationship to the Lord Jesus Christ—He is our Good Shepherd. Because He is, we shall be content.

This passage is one of the more misunderstood statements of Scripture. We usually read one thing and think another. While reading "He maketh me to lie down in green pastures" we are thinking "He *allows* me to lie down in green pastures." Our mind envisions full sheep in a lush meadow, enjoying life to the fullest, literally living off the fat of the land.

But read it again. The action of lying down in green pastures is not occasioned by a sated appetite; the shepherd "makes"—forces—the sheep to lie down. The instigation is *his*, not theirs. If they had their choice, they would not lie down. Not in green pastures! That is the place for eating!

I don't want to lie down in green pastures either! Green pastures symbolize good times. They speak of those days when the sun is shining, birds are singing, and all is well. Green pastures are the very opposite of barren lands; they convey the idea of abundance.

In green pastures we eat well, are healthy, bills are paid, friends are plentiful, and life is simply wonderful. There are things to do, places to go, sights to be seen, thrills to be enjoyed. Since we only go 'round once in life, we want to live in green pastures!

We can hardly believe our ears when we hear the Shepherd say, "Lie down." We cry out, "Not now, Lord! I have too much to do! I just don't have time to lie down!"

But, mister, you had better write it down in capital letters, underline it, and memorize it: when the Shepherd says, "Lie down," you will lie down! Ready or not, you will lie down! Willing or not, you will lie down!

How does He do it? Oh, there could be ten thousand answers to that question. Right in the midst of your activity and busyness, at a time when your schedule is crowded full of meaningful and worthwhile activities, you are forced to stop.

Some of us know the abruptness of hearing a doctor say, "You have cancer." I wanted to say, "Lord, I don't have time for cancer! There is no way that I can crowd it into my schedule!" But God said, "Lie down! I want to talk with you for a while!"

It has often been said that many a man will not look up until he is flat on his back. And we who know the Lord may even get so busy working for Him that He has to make us "lie down in green pastures." Then we remember who the Shepherd is!

We are odd creatures—we know things that we

refuse to learn! We know that the Lord is our Shepherd, and that we are totally dependent on Him. But we have not leaned that we need Him in green pastures. "Who needs a shepherd when the grass is green and plentiful?" we unconsciously think. And for our own good, we have to learn that blessings come from Him.

"For who maketh thee to differ from another? And what hast thou that thou didst not receive? Now if thou didst receive it, why dost thou glory, as if thou hadst not received it?" (I Corinthians 4:7).

It's amazing how quickly we can put a demanding schedule aside when we are called to stand beside the still form of a loved one. We, who were so busy that we didn't have time to eat a meal with our own family, suddenly forget the job. Whether for a day, three days, or two weeks, we see that God is in charge, and we obey His command to "lie down in green pastures."

When your business gets to going so well that you have no time at all for God and His Church, don't be surprised when the Lord tells you to lie down. The Good Shepherd loves you so much that He would rather see you go bankrupt than to lose your soul over an office, or a store, or a farm. Jesus asked, "For what shall it profit a man, if he shall gain the whole world, and lose his own soul?" (Mark 8:36).

I do not want to oversimplify the issue and imply that God says, "Lie down," only when we are more concerned with the grass than with the Shepherd. The apostle Paul was forced to lie down lest he "should be exalted above measure through the abundance of the revelation" given unto him (II Corinthians 12:7). A man born blind was made to lie down "that the works of God should be made manifest in him" (John 9:3).

Nearly a decade ago my wife was compelled to lie down with rheumatoid arthritis. Why? We don't know. We do know that God does heal the sick, but why this?

Listen: *is it our place to quibble with the Shepherd?* Can we accuse Him of unfairness simply because we do not understand all His plans? If He explained it to us, could we comprehend the meaning? Was Gethsemane only for Jesus, or should we too pray, "Not my will, Lord, but Thine be done"?

If your Shepherd tells you to lie down, obey Him. Obedience will be contrary to the flesh, but you will discover that it is better to lie down at His command than to enjoy green pastures against His will.

"It is good for me that I have been afflicted," wrote the psalmist (Psalm 119:71). Do you want to argue with him? The apostle Paul wrote, "Most gladly therefore will I rather glory in my infirmities, that the power of Christ may rest upon me" (II Corinthians 12:9).

Do you want to have your soul restored? Then begin by taking time for God. If you do not take the initiative, He will. He will make you lie down, green pastures or not, "till thou know that the Most High ruleth in the kingdom of men" (Daniel 4:25).

# WHEN
## THE DOCTOR SAYS,
## "YOU HAVE CANCER"

(More than four years ago God forced me to "lie down" with cancer. A few weeks later I wrote the following testimony, which appeared in the *Pentecostal Evangel.*)

You realize that it happens every day, but you seldom think about it; for you never dream it might someday happen to you. But when your doctor looks you in the eye and says, "*You have cancer,*" your whole world changes.

*Cancer* is an ugly word. It connotes death. Oh, not all who are afflicted with cancer die of that malady. You know that. But you cannot disassociate cancer and dying; and you think about it when your physician sends you to a specialist who takes a biopsy and gives the verdict: "You have cancer."

I know. I have been there. Only a few weeks ago I heard those startling words. They were startling indeed, for I was taken completely by surprise. Malignancy was found inside my mouth and in one side of my neck. Radical surgery would be necessary, and it was to be done right away.

Bang! Just like that! Something hits you in the pit of the stomach! You walk out to the car, start the motor, and just sit there—thinking. *Cancer—that's what he said! Now what? Where do I go from here? Is this the beginning of the end? Will I soon be in eternity? Have I lived my life?*

I'm no pessimist or fatalist. I enjoy living so much that I long ago decided never to admit to more than twenty-three years! Both by nature and disposition I look on the bright side. I try to avoid being around people who have a morbid outlook. Chronic complainers find me a poor listener.

Yet when the news of cancer came, thoughts of fatalism, pessimism, and gloom began knocking at the door of my mind.

But—and I say this entirely to the glory of God—the gospel I have had the privilege of preaching for nearly a quarter of a century actually worked! When the crisis came, God was there! I didn't sit in the car a long time, praying, asking God why. There were no tears. Instead victory—supernatural, transcendent victory—flooded my soul, and I found myself thanking God for trusting me with a new experience. The thought of seeing Jesus face-to-face was exciting! And before Satan could plant any seeds of depression, the Lord chased him away.

Maybe I sound like a fool, but before God I tell you the truth: from the first day I heard about having cancer to this present day, I have not been beset by fear, doubt, or depression. In fact, I recall saying to my wife one day, "What's the matter with me? I don't feel like people are supposed to feel who have cancer." God has been so very gracious and has given peace *in* (not from!) the storm. What do people do who don't know the Lord?

When Satan saw that the thought of dying did not terrify me, he came up with two other arguments to cause discouragement. But the Holy Spirit gave the answer each time and closed the devil's mouth!

The enemy said, "What if an operation on your face leaves you looking grotesque? Would you stand before a congregation like that?"

And the Holy Spirit said, "Remember Paul? Was he handsome? And besides, preacher, look in the mirror again. Maybe an operation would help. What have you got to lose?" The Bible does not say this, but it definitely works: "Laugh at the devil, and he will flee from you."

Then Satan said, "What if it takes your voice? What good is a preacher without a voice?" The Holy Spirit answered, "In spite of your lack of education, I have already given you a pen that is reaching farther than your voice ever could."

After those three suggestions—that of dying, that of horrible scars, and that of losing my voice—the enemy left me alone. He may be back tomorrow; but to this day he has not made another attempt to discourage or depress me. Thank God!

I asked for one month's delay in the operation. The wonderful people of my congregation went to fasting and prayer. Somehow the news spread. Every day there were cards, letters, and phone calls—all saying, "We're praying for you! Everything will be all right!" Often while reading gracious words of encouragement I wept. "Why, Lord, should so many people care?" When I get to heaven, I want that question answered!

As the date for the operation drew near, God gave the assurance that I would have to go through it, but that everything would indeed be all right. And it was!

I don't want to bore you with details. Suffice it to say that the operation lasted six hours. The scheduled skin graft inside my mouth was unnecessary because the cancer (about as big around as a quarter) came out without roots! Although the jugular vein, the broad muscle, and all glands were taken out of one side of my neck, I didn't even need a blood transfusion!

That night I asked for and was given permission to get out of bed! Four days later, the doctor said, "You might as well go on home." Two weeks later, I was back in the pulpit preaching the gospel! And no one has turned away in horror because of my looks! God has answered somebody's prayer.

It would take a long time to tell you all the specifics of the miracles that took place in my body and mind. I am actually thankful that God allowed the operation. You see, now there is no mistake about it; I had cancer. And the spiritual victories that were given could not have come in any other way. Had God taken the cancer away as soon as it was discovered, I always would have wondered if the doctors made a mistake in their diagnosis. Now I know it was for real.

The Holy Spirit has been speaking to my heart during the past few weeks in a way that has changed my life. It all began when the doctor said, "You have cancer!" May I share some of the "blessings of cancer" with you?

1. When the doctor says, "you have cancer," you think about dying. That is good. We need to seriously consider the solemn fact that our days on earth could end at any moment. There is something about the ordinary routine of living that tends to mesmerize us into thinking that we are going to live forever. "Tomorrow shall be as this day, and much more abundant." The news of cancer gives a much-needed jolt to that kind of thinking and brings us face-to-face with the reality of death.

2. When the doctor says, "You have cancer," you see time in its true perspective. You suddenly see that there is nothing to live for in the realm called time. "A vapor, that appeareth for a little time, and then vanisheth away"—that is our life. Time offers no sure footing, no solid foundation, no enduring hopes. Everything that can be seen with the eye or touched with the hand will someday be burned up. The things that are seen are temporal. So really it is eternity, not time, that is the true determining factor for everything.

3. When the doctor says, "You have cancer," the past is reviewed in a new light. What have I accomplished in life? Oh, I've had some days of

happiness, but what kind of mark have I left? What good have I done? Is the world any better for my being here? If I could only go back and live some of those days over. . . .

4. When the doctor says, "You have cancer," the "now" becomes all-important. You can't relive the past; you're not sure of the future; so take full advantage of the now. God will give you only twenty-four hours a day—no more, no less. Use every one of them. Time is too valuable to waste. Every day is a gracious gift. Every sunrise is a miracle. There is no time to sit and mope; what living you're going to do had better be done today!

5. When the doctor says, "You have cancer," the opinions of others mean nothing. They may misunderstand your motives, but you will not hold that against them. *You know* there are wrongs to be righted, confessions to be made, and old grudges to be settled. You can't afford to lie about anything. "What do I care what others think? Tomorrow I may be in eternity!"

6. When the doctor says, "You have cancer," devils try to invade your mind. You quickly learn about the reality of the underworld. It existed all along, but you had never been brought to a confrontation with it. You are now forced to deal with demons of fear, depression, doubt, torment, confusion, and hatred. Is that bad? Think about this: would you rather defeat them in this world or contend with them in the world to come?

7. When the doctor says, "You have cancer," you

are tempted to question God. That is good. One of the unkindest things we ever do to the Almighty is to ignore Him. Go ahead and question Him; but be ready: He has the answers!

"Where was God when I was afflicted with this terrible thing?" That is easy—He was in the same place as when His Son was being nailed to the tree. He did not send cancer upon you, but He did allow it. He is interested in where you will spend eternity—never forget that! And "all things"— including cancer—"work together for good to them that love God."

8. When the doctor says, "You have cancer," you need more than human help. I would be the worst of ingrates to speak disparagingly of doctors. Their skill and knowledge astound me. I am a debtor to the many men who have spent so many years in research. I admire them; I respect and honor them.

But in spite of all their ingenuity, when you hear the word *cancer*, you know your life is in the hands of God. As your cot is rolled into the operating room, you know that soon you will be unconscious and surgery will begin. The only way you can face that moment with confidence is to have Jesus Christ living in your heart.

"But," you say, "I *have* prayed! When I found out that I had cancer, I prayed—but God wasn't there!" God wasn't there? Sure He was! Let me ask, What were you praying for? Only for your healing? No wonder you did not get an answer. God wants *you!*

"Well, if God will just heal me, I'll serve Him." If

that is your attitude, you might as well forget the whole thing. God is not in the bargaining business. He wants you to surrender your heart to Him—whether you're ever healed or not.

"But what if He doesn't heal me?" Would that be awful? You would wake up in heaven! To be absent from the body is to be present with the Lord. "I have a desire to depart and to be with the Lord, which is far better," the apostle said. "To me to live is Christ, and to die is gain."

9. When your doctor says, "You have cancer," you come face-to-face with what life is all about. Now you have a choice. Are you going to throw away this, the greatest moment of your life?

# BESIDE
## STILL WATERS

"He leadeth me beside the still waters." This, one of the more beautiful phrases of Scripture, is seldom read "as is." A host of tradition has clouded our vision. We remember pictures of sheep peacefully drinking from a gently flowing brook. With that picture in mind, we add two things which the Bible does not say: There is nothing mentioned in the Word about drinking the water, and there is nothing in Scripture about a gently flowing brook.

Now, those truths are wonderful and may be taught from other Biblical principles. But they are not part of Psalm 23:2. Read it again. He leads me *beside* the water, and the water is *still*.

This is the trouble with our human logic: we try to outguess God! Our "profound" reasoning says, "Well, if God leads us beside still waters, isn't it for the purpose of getting a drink? Isn't that what water is for?" And so, in ignoring the simple and powerful phraseology of the Holy Spirit, we once again focus on our desires and miss altogether our Shepherd's intentions.

First, let's settle the matter of the condition of the water. The Bible says, "*still* waters." The old adage that "still waters run deep" simply is not true; still waters do not run at all! Had the Holy Spirit meant fresh waters or pure waters or refreshing waters or lifegiving waters He could have used any of those adjectives. He said rather, "still waters," so we may safely assume that He meant still waters.

"But," someone says, "still waters get stagnant!" There you go again, trying to fit divine revelation into the test tube of human logic! Just read what it says, not what you think it means!

I have read many, many pages on this passage, and every writer matter-of-factly introduces a subject which God does not introduce. Immediately, men start discussing getting a drink. And that brings up the subject of thirst. And away we go! Chapter after chapter discusses the thirst of the soul and the inadequacies of earth's "waters" to satisfy.

But listen, the inspired statement is, "He leadeth me *beside* the still waters." Where? Beside them, not to them or out in them but beside them! Once again, human reason hinders divine revelation. We say, "Why else would thirsty sheep be led beside waters?"

We just won't quit, will we? Where did we get the idea that this sheep is thirsty? It is dangerous to develop the habit of reading things like that into Scripture. Such logic is foundational to false doctrines.

Think about this: *still waters form a mirror, and when we stand beside them we see ourselves!*

Now that's simple, isn't it? Yet it is exactly what the psalmist was saying. It happens *after* the sheep is made to lie down in green pastures and *before* his soul is restored. This explains the purpose of the command to "lie down!" And it outlines the plan for restoration.

A man has got to see himself! Until he sees himself as God sees him, his life will be totally out of perspective. And he cannot see himself aright until God stops him.

"Still waters" represent the Word. Hear the admonition of James: "If any be a hearer of the word, and not a doer, he is like unto a man beholding his natural face in a glass: For he beholdeth himself, and goeth his way, and straightway forgetteth what manner of man he was. But whoso looketh into the perfect law of liberty, and continueth therein, he being not a forgetful hearer, but a doer of the work, this man shall be blessed in his deed" (James 1:23-25).

A curious thing happens as you approach still waters. At first you see distant trees and hills outlined perfectly in the water—all upside down! You see a topsy-turvey world. Everything is inverted.

As you draw nearer, the inverted world diminishes and the heavens begin to fill the scene.

But when you stand beside still waters you see yourself in heaven's backdrop! And that's the way a man needs to see himself. Otherwise, we will continually be comparing ourselves with others, and will fall "short of the glory" (Romans 3:23).

You are a creature of eternity, and you do not see yourself as you are until you see yourself in that light. Your soul—your mind—can never be restored until you see yourself as you are.

The scene is never beautiful. How can it be? I crucified Jesus. I drove the nails in His hands. I spat in His face. And I have not lived up to the consecration that I made to Him. The picture is ugly. It brings me to my knees.

Now I am beginning to see why He stopped me when all was going well. "In my prosperity I said, I shall never be moved" (Psalm 30:6). For my own good, God had to throw up a blockade in my path. I was so busy that I forgot who I am, where I came from, and where I am going.

But a miracle begins beside the still waters. Understand me when I say it, when I see myself as I should, I see God. And though I may not fully understand, I gladly rejoice in the knowledge that He is doing what is best for me.

# THE
## RESTORED
### SOUL

"He restoreth my soul." With this simple yet sublime statement, the psalmist makes a twofold transition. *First*, it now begins to be apparent that he is not talking about sheep, but about men. While it may be true that sheep need, on occasion, to have some kind of restoration, the obvious truth is about God's dealings with His people. The picture of the sheep remains, but at this point it becomes an obvious parable.

*Second*, with these few words, "He restoreth my soul," the inspired writer moves from the natural to the supernatural, from the mundane to the miraculous. Any old shepherd can lead sheep beside still waters. These are run-of-the-mill events which may be accomplished by anyone who is genuinely interested in acquiring the skills of a shepherd.

But to restore the soul—that is another matter! Shepherds don't restore souls! For, when you come right down to it, shepherds cannot really communicate with sheep. Habits may force patterns of behavior, but men and sheep are of two different orders, and one cannot communicate with the other.

The Psalm is a parable. Its vital sequence continues. After I am forced to lie down when I didn't want to, after I am led to the reflecting still waters where I see myself as God sees me, I cry out for the restoration of my soul. At that point I need an inward miracle—one which can be performed only by my Good Shepherd.

Before we can intelligently discuss the restoration of the soul, we must ask, "What is a soul?"

Man is a tripartite being. The Bible teaches that we consist of "spirit and soul and body" (I Thessalonians 5:23). Your spirit is the God-likeness in you, and ever allures you to follow the right, the good, and the true. Your body is the Adam-likeness in you, and draws your attention to the temporal, the earthly, and carnal. Surrender to your spirit and you will be led to life. Surrender to your body and you will be led to death.

"For to be carnally minded is death; but to be spiritually minded is life and peace" (Romans 8:6). Note the expressions of the apostle, for in this verse he defines the soul. He did not speak of being either carnal or spiritual, but of being carnally *minded* or spiritually *minded*.

The soul is the mind. It is between the spirit and the body. The spirit cannot influence the body, nor can the body make any impression on the spirit. These two are at warfare (Galatians 5:6—which should read *spirit* instead of *Spirit*) with each other. And the battleground is the mind!

God, operating through my spirit, seeks to

influence my mind. And Satan, working through my body, seeks to influence my mind. Understand this clearly: as the mind goes, so goes the whole person. Your mind is you!

"He restoreth my soul." He restores my mind. It needs restoration from time to time. The tensions, the frustrations, the anxieties which result from the continual crossfire in my mind call for outside assistance. I can't solve my own problems. I need a mediator.

Man can't help. Psychologists, psychiatrists, and psychoanalysts are of no more benefit than astrologists, palm readers, and crystal ball gazers. Their motives are apparent—when you start to leave! I need help that is not affected by the carnal.

Only Jesus restores the mind. He wipes away all the cobwebs of time, and as I stand "beside the still waters" He brings my thinking back into focus. I see myself in heaven's backdrop, and suddenly the things of time fade into insignificance. Why should I, a creature of eternity, devote myself so fervently to things that will someday be burned up? "For a man's life consisteth not in the abundance of the things which he possesseth" (Luke 12:15).

The apostle Paul admonishes saints not to be "conformed to this world: but be ye transformed by the renewing of your mind" (Romans 12:2). It happens in the mind, the soul. You are "transformed" when you start thinking right.

Victories are won and defeats are suffered in the mind—not in the body, or in the spirit, but in the mind. Let your flesh triumph in battle and you have only created a severer turmoil in your spirit. Let your spirit win a conflict and your body will vehemently oppose it. But when your mind wins, the battleground is cleared!

It goes without saying, of course, that when a man's mind is restored he follows his spirit in the Godward way. He does so, however, not by coercion but by choice.

To "restore" means to "give back." Man needs his mind back. He lost it through sin. Satan got a hook in man's mental jaw when he sinned, and he hasn't been able to think clearly ever since. He needs his mind back. His spirit will give him no rest until he is able to do his own thinking again.

You see, here is one of the basic differences between the workings of God and Satan. God wants you free.

Satan, on the other hand, wants to usurp your brain. He does not want you to think. He wants to control you completely, and his only way of getting at you is through your body with its five senses.

Since we, as Christians, continue to struggle with the flesh—and that conflict will continue as long as we live—there are times when we sin (I John 1:8, 10). And when we do, our mind is captured. It will be impossible to have a proper perspective until our Shepherd restores our soul.

This miracle can happen for you every time you need it. You will not worry God. He delights in your calling upon Him for help.

But don't expect this miracle of soul restoration to take place at the drop of a knee. God may slow you down for a while. He may make you look yourself over in the light of the Word.

This is not an act of penance; it is done to prepare you for a mighty miracle: God wants to give your mind back to you! Do you want it? "If the Son therefore shall make you free, ye shall be free indeed" (John 8:36). "He restoreth my soul."

# FROM
# PASTURES
## TO PATHS

"For precept must be upon precept, precept upon precept; line upon line, line upon line; here a little, and there a little" (Isaiah 28:19). So God reveals Himself to His people.

How beautifully our Lord's care for His own is gradually unfolded in the twenty-third Psalm! After two statements of faith and confidence, in verse one, the revelation of God's method begins. I was in green pastures, and I loved it. My time was spent in gorging myself. The bountiful blessings catered to my every whim. But God said, "Lie down!" I tried to turn Him off; I didn't want to lie down. I was too busy for an operation. My schedule was so full that I didn't have time to be flat on my back for a few weeks. But I discovered that when God says, "Lie down!" you will lie down!

After slowing me down, after stopping me, the Lord led me beside still waters. I looked into the reflecting mirror of those motionless waters and the sight I saw was not pleasant. I saw myself in heaven's backdrop, and I was ugly. I had been in green pastures so long I was as fat as a pig. My jowls were so full my eyes looked like two little peepholes sunk in a sea of lard. I had been living only for myself, and it showed!

I cried for help! I knew what had been going on but was powerless to help myself. "O wretched man that I am! who shall deliver me from the body of this death?" (Romans 7:24). *There's a dead body tied to me, and I am not free to do what I know is right! All this foolish body can see is another delicious tuft of grass, and it goes after it. I'm destroying myself and am helpless to stop.*

Then my wonderful Shepherd, the Lord Jesus Christ, performs a miracle. "He restoreth my soul." He sets my thinking straight. . . . He "makes me free from the law of sin and death" (Romans 8:2). "Knowing this, that our old man is crucified with him, that the body of sin might be destroyed, that henceforth we should not serve sin. For he that is dead is freed from sin" (Romans 6:6, 7).

Now, with a restored mind, I can "walk in newness of life" (Romans 6:2). "All things are become new" (II Corinthians 5:17). And my Shepherd leads me.

The experience itself was frustrating. At times I wondered where God is. To be very honest, there were a few times I wondered if there actually is a God! I didn't understand what was going on, and it confused me. But now He is leading, and all the turmoil of the test causes me to thank Him for caring so very much.

"He leadeth me in the paths of righteousness." What a contrast! Once I wanted only pastures; now

He is leading me in paths. In pastures He makes me lie down. In paths He leads me.

Pastures speak of the gratification of the flesh. They are those places and times when we live only for ourselves. *Our* desires, *our* aims, *our* ambitions, *our* needs, *our* wishes, *our* hankerings—pastures cater to these things. The emphasis is always on self and its whims.

Let's not kid ourselves, we love pastures! Every man does. It's nice to enjoy plenty, and to live without severe crises. Sunshine is pleasant, and no one in his right mind would prefer a tornado to a balmy day.

Pastures, however, have one serious drawback: they don't lead anywhere! There are no goals beyond the present, no visions of a better world to come, no ambitions for the future. Life is reduced to the simplest basics: *here is a nice tuft of grass—eat it! And there is another—eat it!* Men in pastures live like animals; "there is no past, there is no future, there is only the now. Enjoy it."

After we stand beside still waters, pastures do not satisfy. That view of ourselves in heaven's backdrop changed the whole scene. There we saw ourselves as creatures of eternity, and time can no longer satisfy. We were created in God's image and likeness, so why live for green grass? The foolishness of earth became apparent when our mind was restored.

Now our Shepherd leads us in paths. Paths have a beginning and an end. They are not aimless. If a man who is lost can find a path, he no longer wanders. He knows the path will lead him out.

We are headed toward another world. Wallowing in green pastures on this planet will not prepare us for that life in the beyond. We need a plain path, and we need a Guide. "This one thing I do, forgetting those things which are behind, and reaching forth unto those things which are before, I press toward the mark for the prize of the high calling of God in Christ Jesus" (Philippians 3:13, 14).

Lord, ever correct me when I stray into self-gratifying pastures. Do whatever is necessary to turn my vision heavenward. Help me remember that the way of the Cross leads home. "Teach me thy way, O Lord, and lead me in a plain path" (Psalm 27:11).

# "HE LEADETH ME"

"He leadeth me in the paths of righteousness for his name's sake" (Psalm 23:3). This well-known statement answers six important questions about the Christian's day-by-day relationship to his Lord: *who, what, how, where, why,* and *when?*

1. *Who?*

Who leads me? This is as vital a decision as man will ever make. We all play "follow-the-leader," but it's not a game. It's for real! Wherever our leader goes, we go. Since we are on a sure road to another world, and since that next world is eternal, and since that eternity is composed of either unending joy or unending torment, we need the right leader.

Our leader must know the road. And there is only one way for anyone to know a road: he must have traveled over it before! I am on an itinerary that heads toward a cemetery. Yet innately I know that the tombstone is not the end. Death does not mark the cessation of my existence. I need a leader who knows the way through the tunnel marked "death."

Only One qualifies. His name is Jesus. He has been through death. In life He was "in all points tempted like as we are" (Hebrews 4:14). In death

He was Victor, coming out of the tomb with "the keys of hell and of death" (Revelation 1:18).

Ask these two questions of any who would offer to be your leader: "Have you lived tomorrow yet?" and "Have you been through death?" Only Jesus can answer both queries in the affirmative. So follow Him!

2. *What?*

"He leadeth me." He cares about me. The One "who is the image of the invisible God, the firstborn of every creature" (Colossians 1:15) is concerned with my individual needs. When a tear comes to my eye, He sees it—and He is ready to be my Friend. When I feel so weak that I cannot walk, He takes my hand and helps me along. When the night is so dark that all hope seems gone, He floods my soul with a light brighter than the noonday sun.

He leadeth me! It is a personal relationship. We must beware of the concept that "He leadeth *us.*" Such a thesis lets us hide away in the crowd, just an insignificant part of the group. And it also presupposes that our Shepherd leads all His sheep the same way.

But not so! Being members of "the body of Christ" does not keep us from being "members in particular" (I Corinthians 12:27). Each one of us needs individual leading. Do not judge your brother simply because he does not walk in your footsteps. His Shepherd is leading him, and you must not assume that God deals with each of His own in exactly the same way. "Who art thou that judgest another man's servant? to his own master he standeth or falleth" (Romans 14:4).

What is your Shepherd doing? "He which hath begun a good work in you will perform it until the day of Jesus Christ" (Philippians 1:6). He is finishing your salvation.

3. *How?*

How does my heavenly Shepherd minister to my needs? He does so by leading me. He walks along in front of me and shows me the way. He does not coerce. He delivers no blistering lectures. He does not drive. He leads.

Jesus lived on earth to be our Example. When we come to the place we feel we can go no farther, we see His footprints. We see the traces of blood. And we hear His voice, saying, "Follow me" (Matthew 4:19). Courage rises, and we follow.

It is important to remember that our Leader never asks us to explore, to venture into the unknown. He is not an astute Potentate who demands more of His subjects than of Himself. He is our Leader. And we will follow Him wherever He goes.

4. *Where?*

Where does He lead? He leads into paths of righteousness—into right paths. The right path is the one that leads to the desired destination. All others are wrong; they may be beautiful, but they are wrong, for they do not take us where we want to go.

Pity the man who judges his life by the scenery

along the way! The Lord never promised to lead us down a lush lane. Never! He said He would lead us down *the right road.*

The right road is sometimes rocky. It is oft a barren way. It goes through wilderness places, through the Slough of Despond, through Vanity-fair, through Doubting Castle, and through the Valley of the Shadow of Death. This is no easy road. But it is the right road!

Depend on it, the right road goes through Gethsemane. There's a cross in the middle of this path. And you can't detour around it! Stay on the right road and you will be crucified!

Jesus calls this right path "narrow" and "strait" (Matthew 7:13, 14). As a matter of fact, you can't even find this way by yourself. You need someone to show it to you, and only Jesus can do it—for He is the Way! Without this Leader, you are lost forever.

5. *Why?*

"For his name's sake." God has an interest in you. And He is doing all He can to protect His investment.

The whole purpose of the road is that it lead to the proper destination. Jesus wants to lead you on the only way that will get your soul to heaven. He is more interested in your eternity than in your now.

For you, He left the portals of glory. For you, He "took upon him the form of a servant, and was made in the likeness of men: And being found in fashion as a man, he humbled himself, and became obedient unto death, even the death of the cross"

(Philippians 2:7, 8). Now, after paying a price like that, your Lord is not going to sit idly by and let you stray away; He will exert every pressure at His command to keep you in His fold.

The battle of the ages is between God and Satan. And the present victories for one side or the other take place in the souls of men. Satan wants you because he hates God. God wants you because He loves you.

"For his name's sake." His name is Jesus. Jesus means Savior. Our Lord is what He is: He is Savior! His name is at stake in your salvation. All of heaven's reputation is laid on the line for you! God cares that much for you!

6. *When?*

When does all this glorious leading take place? Am I to wait until I enter the world to come before I can enjoy the blessings of divine and personal concern over every detail of my well-being?

No! "He leadeth me"—present progressive tense! It is taking place right now—today! We miss many of God's richest blessings because we yield to the subtle suggestion of Satan that true religion only has to do with the dim distant future. And because we become weary of waiting, we fall into sin.

But you don't have to wait! Your eternal life has already begun. Your heavenly Father knows your blood pressure. He orders your every heartbeat! "He careth for you" (I Peter 5:7). He wants to lead you NOW.

We must, however, warn you that His leading only affects those who follow—and continue to follow. We are not puppets on a string. Salvation is for "whosoever will" (John 3:16). You have a will. Use it to follow your heavenly Shepherd today.

# THE COMMON DENOMINATOR

"Yea, though I walk through the valley of the shadow of death, I will fear no evil: for thou art with me."

The pattern never varies. Just as soon as the mind of the believer is restored and he begins to be led in right paths, he bursts out in praise. And the basis of his praise invariably is about the victory over the fear of death.

Before the transformation beside the still waters, the silly pilgrim offered exuberant praise only for the most juvenile things, such as prosperity, good health, and earthly success. In those days of mere elementary development in Christ his rapture followed the ebb and flow of carnal blessings. Like a child, he was happy when he got what he wanted and he pouted when he didn't.

Something transcendent happened, however, as he stood in forced contemplation beside the still waters. There he saw himself as a creature of eternity, and his whole perspective changed. Things of earth which had once seemed so all-important faded into the background. Things which formerly elicited praise and rapture were viewed as they really are—cheap, temporal, and unworthy of the affection of the child of God. "For the fashion of this world passeth away" (I Corinthians 7:31).

And for the first time in his life, he looked at death. Most people shy away from any consideration of that time when life as we now know it will come to an end. To the natural man, death is an ugly, fearsome spectre. Knowing that he will someday die, he refuses to talk about it or to think about it. He knows that ignoring it will not make it go away, but he ignores it anyhow.

Let the natural man stand beside the still, cold form of a loved one. The message comes through loud and clear: he knows that his time is coming, and innately he knows that death is not a cessation of existence.

But he walks away, wipes the tears from his eyes, and forgets! He has to! If he did not forget, the weight of the contemplation would drive him to insanity.

Death is the end of life on earth. It is the stepping out of this body into some kind of another life in some kind of another world. And that other world is eternal. Every man has the inborn consciousness that the world to come has a vital link with this one—that the world to come is either reward or retribution.

Death is the common denominator among us all. The Preacher of Old Testament times said, "And how dieth the wise man? as the fool" (Ecclesiastes 2:16). At that moment when the heart stops beating, all former differences disappear. Fame does not stay death's hand. The nobleman may gain a short extension of days on earth by a blood transfusion—from a peasant! Or it could be the other way around: the nobleman's blood may be given to the peasant!

This thing called death, which is but the cessation of this thing called life, puts every man on the same level. One bullet will kill the doctor of philosophy, and one bullet will kill the idiot. Let a thousand people drink poisoned water and a thousand people will die. Social caste will be of no avail.

Death plays no favorites. The mere fact that some may live longer than others is an absolute facade. Nobody cheats death! And to ask the hundred-year-old man about the secret of his long life must surely be done tongue-in-cheek! Put one hundred years in the balance with eternity, then put twenty years in the balance with eternity, and you will not be able to tell the difference between those two life-spans.

Death is that experience of stepping from time into eternity. It awaits us all. "But after this the judgment" (Hebrews 9:27). Therefore the most important day of any man's life is the day of his death. That moment will determine his eternity.

There is only one way to be ready to face death. You need to have a close friend who has been there—someone who has been through the experience, who has been to both divisions of the world to come, and who knows the route to heaven.

You need Jesus! He alone has conquered death.

He alone can lead you through that experience from which the flesh flees in horror. He alone can cause you to sing in the awful night. He alone can make you sing about death!

To say that you believe Jesus is the Son of God is not sufficient. "The devils also believe and tremble" (James 2:19). "Ye must be born again" (John 3:7).

Yes, you will die. That is the common denominator among us. When you leave this life you will enter another one—that is inevitable. But which world: heaven or hell? That is the decision you are making today. You are making your choice.

You can be in the category described through the wise man of old. Through him God said, "Because I have called, and ye refused; I have stretched out my hand, and no man regarded; but ye have set at nought all my counsel, and would none of my reproof: I also will laugh at your calamity; I will mock when your fear cometh" (Proverbs 1:24-26).

Or you can join the psalmist who sang, "Yea, though I walk through the valley of the shadow of death, I will fear no evil" (Psalm 23:4).

Personal faith in Jesus makes the difference.

# ECLIPSED

A psalm is a song. The Biblical book of Psalms is a collection of divinely inspired songs preserved thousands of years. As a young man Jesus sang them. And He knew, as no one else can know, that the Holy Spirit Himself was the Author of each phrase.

Our Lord sang, "Yea, though I walk through the valley of the shadow of death...." As He did, He understood the multiple truths contained in such few and simple words.

This thing men call death is a *walk*—it is not a lying down. It is a walking *through*—not merely into; not a stopping point. Death is a walk *through a valley*—there is another world beyond.

But the curious phrase used by the psalmist, and later verified by Jesus Himself, is the statement "the shadow of death." Speaking as one who had been restored by the grace of God, the Old Testament singer refused to call death death. Sinners may experience death, but the believer walks through death's shadow!

During His ministry, our Lord once used exactly the same expression. It follows His parable of the unjust steward in Luke 16. Verse 9 reads, "And I say unto you, Make to yourselves friends of the mammon of unrighteousness; that, when ye fail, they may receive you into everlasting habitations."

The warning "when ye fail" speaks of the thing men call death. But the literal reading is "when ye suffer an eclipse." Isn't that what the psalmist said—"the shadow of death"?

The dictionary defines "eclipse" as "the total or partial obscuring of one heavenly body by another; also, a passing into the shadow of a heavenly body."

You have seen a celestial eclipse. You have watched the moon pass into the earth's shadow. Or you have watched the moon make such a shadow as to blot out the sun. During the eclipse of the moon you knew that the moon continued to exist; it was merely in a shadow. During the eclipse of the sun you knew that the blazing orb which lights the earth had not gone out; you were merely in a shadow.

When my heart stops beating—if Jesus tarries—I will not die; I will experience an eclipse. I will pass into the shadow of a heavenly Body. Jesus died for me, therefore I do not have to die. Oh, this body will wear out and will be placed in a grave, but I will not die! "Death is swallowed up in victory" (I Corinthians 15:54). My Savior satisfied absolute righteousness, therefore I can shout, "O death, where is thy sting? O grave, where is thy victory? The sting of death is sin; and the strength of sin is the law. But thanks be to God, which giveth us the victory through our Lord Jesus Christ" (I Corinthians 15:55-57).

Should I go on and you remain, you may look at the still form of the house in which I lived for a while. However, I will not be in that casket. I will be "with Christ; which is far better" (Philippians 1:23). But you cannot see me; I will be eclipsed from your sight. If you should want to know about me then, ask Jesus.

Though I will be eclipsed from your sight by the thing called death, I will fear no evil. Having faith in the Christ of Calvary, I know that the best world is yet to come.

Jesus used this same expression one other time, and in so doing He laid down the qualification for the glorious hope beyond the grave. He said to Peter, "Simon, Simon, behold, Satan hath desired to have you, that he may sift you as wheat: But I have prayed for thee, that thy faith fail not"—that thy faith may not suffer an eclipse (Luke 22:31, 32)!

The alternatives are real. If your faith suffers an eclipse you will pass into eternal death. But if your faith cannot be shaded you will never die; you will be eclipsed by Jesus!

If you can say, "For thou art with me," you can also say, "I will fear no evil." Our Lord holds the keys of death.

# COMFORTED

"Thy rod and thy staff they comfort me." The sheep is now rejoicing. He has every reason to shout. His shepherd is a good one—one who loves and cares for his sheep, one who disciplines them when necessary (but always in love), one who stays with them even in the face of eminent death. Total trust in, and total submission to, the shepherd has produced calm and confidence within the sheep.

The picture, of course, is a parallel. Jesus is the good Shepherd, and we are the sheep of His pasture. His care and concern for us is never-ending. Again and again we have witnessed how He has led us through the most difficult places. We thought He was cruel when He made us lie down in green pastures; we were repulsed by the reflection of ourselves which we saw beside the still waters. We wondered, "What kind of Shepherd is this? Doesn't He love us at all? Why all this unpleasantness?

Then He restored our mind. He began to lead us in right paths. And now we do not fear even death, so long as He is with us!

Everything has changed. "Old things are passed away; behold, all things are become new" (II

Corinthians 5:17). We have miraculously come to a place which we never thought possible: we actually thank Him for the comfort we daily receive from those two ugly sticks in His hand—His rod and His staff!

Every shepherd has them. They are indispensable equipment in the care and protection of sheep. And though every sheep grows accustomed to seeing them, he does not like them—not until by bitter experience he sees their necessity. Then they comfort him.

Some have gone to great lengths to transform these shepherd's tools into types. The rod, they say, speaks of the Word, and the staff, in their analogy, is representative of the Holy Spirit.

Such arguments are, I feel, totally unnecessary. Not only do they break down at too many points (be careful about making too drastic a distinction between the work of the Word and the work of the Spirit), they turn attention away from the Shepherd.

When you read it, do not emphasize the nouns *rod* and *staff*, but the pronouns *thy* rod and *thy* staff. In any other hands these tools hold no meaning for the sheep!

I am not oversimplifying the situation when I insist that these are tools of protection. Basically the rod protects the sheep against any and all outside enemies, and the staff protects the sheep from himself. I need both kinds of help every day. Without it, I cannot be comforted!

The shepherd's rod resembles a club. It has been called "an extension of the owner's right arm." Phillip Keller, in *A Shepherd Looks at Psalm 23*, wrote, "Each shepherd boy, from the time he first starts to tend his father's flock, takes special pride in the selection of a rod and staff exactly suited to his own size and strength. He goes into the bush and selects a young sapling which is dug from the ground. This is carved and whittled down with great care and patience. The enlarged base of the sapling where its trunk joins the roots is shaped into a smooth, rounded head of hard wood. The sapling itself is shaped to exactly fit the owner's hand. After he completes it, the shepherd boy spends hours practicing with this club, learning how to throw it with amazing speed and accuracy. It becomes his main weapon of defense for both himself and his sheep."

Every child of God knows that we are faced with real dangers every day. The devil is not about to give up. He attacks and attacks and attacks and attacks again.

You see, I may look like a lonely, defenseless sheep (and within myself that's all I am), but I've got a Shepherd who cares for me. He's got a weapon in His hand that will repel every cunning onslaught of the wicked one. And I am safe!

This is why I'm not interested in naming the rod. It's *His*, not mine. It fits *His* hand, not mine. *He* uses it, I don't. All I know is what I need to know: my Shepherd has a weapon which will drive back the devil when he attacks me. So I will be content.

The staff, however, has another purpose. It has the familiar hook on one end of it, and is used to protect the sheep from himself.

When I see my Shepherd drive the enemy back, not allowing the wicked one to hurt me, I get bolder than I should. I start walking in a bigger circle, and I get too far from the Shepherd.

That's when He uses His staff to bring me back. Old dumb, blind me, I didn't know the wolf was behind that tree, and in my frolicking I got too close to it. Then I felt something; it was the Shepherd's staff. He hooked it around my leg (or maybe around my neck!), and started drawing me away from the place where I had started.

In my foolishness I said, "What's going on, Lord? I wasn't doing anything wrong!" Then I saw the wolf slinking away, and I fell on my knees and said, "Thank You, Lord, for Your staff." It saved me from awful ruin.

*When the enemy gets too close to me, the Lord uses the rod; He takes care of the devil. When I get too close to the enemy, the Lord uses the staff; He takes care of me.*

Don't strain to put labels on His "rod" and "staff." He has ten thousand ways of protecting you—because He loves you. And only in the place of constant, divine protection can you be comforted.

# GOD'S STRANGE BANQUET ROOM

*"What's a nice person like you doing in a place like this?"* Words like these usually connote the idea of at least a mild rebuke. They form the stuff from which gossip grows. They indicate surprise born of paradox. Better things were expected of you. How could you stoop so low?

Our human logic insists that nice people belong in nice places, and crude people belong in crude places. When an uncouth man is found in the company of utmost refinement, he stands out like a sore thumb. But at least we admire him for his taste; he did have the good sense to elect to be among good people. If we rebuke him at all, it will be for his behavior, not for his choice of friends.

On the other hand, the presence of an immaculate lady of delicate culture in a den of vilest iniquity prompts the query to the mind, if not to the lips, "What's a nice person like you doing in a place like this?" The rebuke, in this situation, would not be for the behavior, but for the selection of company.

The ways of God are, in like manner, a perpetual paradox to both the saved and the unsaved. Neither

Christian nor sinner can comprehend the doings of Deity. "His ways are past finding out" (Romans 11:33).

Who can explain God's reason for defying human rules of propriety in the selection of a banquet room for His redeemed ones? The psalmist was specific: "Thou preparest a table before me in the presence of mine enemies." And the more we consider our high and holy calling, the more we wonder why our heavenly Father spreads His table in such an unlikely place! *What am I doing in a place like this?*

We prefer to eat in the presence of friends. It is easy to relax when we are among "our kind" of people. Tensions are nonexistent. There is laughter, genuine happiness, and an air of tranquillity. Even the digestive processes of the body are at their peak of efficiency. The only danger is of eating too much. So we do.

But to eat in the presence of enemies is a different story. Who can admire a beautiful table knowing that mortal foes are "drawing a bead" on him through the window? Who can swallow his food while dodging spears? How can digestive processes function properly with the heart pounding furiously? No smile comes to the lips, no laughter born of tranquillity fills the air, and nobody takes a nap.

That, sir, is the picture which your Bible paints. "Thou preparest a table before me in the presence of mine enemies." And when God uses the word "enemies" He means what He says. You live in an unfriendly world! Dispose, at once, of any idea of spiritual relaxation in this body. You can no more be at ease in this life than you can enjoy a steak dinner in the presence of furious headhunters!

Failure to understand this basic principle of the Christian life can easily lead to utter defeat. Life is a battle, not a banquet. It is a warfare, not a vacation. We must, we *must*, we must hear and heed the divine directive to "take unto you the whole armour of God, that ye may be able to withstand in the evil day, and having done all, to stand" (Ephesians 6:13). Relax, sir, and you're dead!

We are, in fact, like Israel in the wilderness. God taught them, in no uncertain terms, that they were in alien territory. For forty years they were instructed in a fundamental truth which is pertinent to this very hour: *each day exposes a new enemy!* And that new enemy will not be ignored; he will defeat you if you do not defeat him!

Young converts need to know that surrender to Christ is not an immediate transfer to utopia. Blessings abound, yes, but the enemy is still very much alive—and his anger is seven times hotter than ever before. The struggle has only begun.

God emphasized this truth to me during this writing. A young man knocked at the door and was welcomed into my study. In his hand was a four-page written testimony; he was afraid he wouldn't remember it all.

One month ago he and his wife responded to the

divine invitation, kneeling at God's altar in surrender to Him. Though raised in church they had turned from their early training and had become dope addicts. They asked, that night, for divine deliverance and rejoiced in the confidence that the Lord had answered their prayer.

The next evening they sat in my study, exuberant in their newfound faith. They vowed to get rid of all their paraphernalia of dope and to begin a new way of living.

But they failed to realize that God's banquet table is in the presence of enemies! And they began to return to their former ways. They hadn't intended to, but they did.

Last night God intervened again, actually taking that young man instantly off one of his highest highs! He cried out to God, and He heard him! Now the family has returned to the heavenly feast, but this time they know where the table is—it's in the presence of enemies! And that awareness is more than half the battle! Satan has the advantage only over those who are "ignorant of his devices" (II Corinthians 2:11).

Paradox of all paradoxes, miracle of all miracles, we can actually enjoy transcendent peace at God's table, even in the presence of enemies! Saints can sing in prison. They offer praise on Patmos. They sleep the night before their execution. Why? Because "the Lord is my shepherd," therefore I will be content. "I will fear no evil: for thou art with me; thy rod and thy staff they comfort me."

I know the enemy is watching, snarling and drooling. He knows that I know, and that makes him more furious than ever. But he can't touch me; my life is hid with Christ in God. Jesus is the Author of my salvation; He will also be its Finisher.

# ENEMIES

"Thou preparest a table before me in the presence of mine enemies." Saints live in alien territory. And the natives are not friendly! Each move they make is calculated to contribute to the ultimate overthrow of those whose names are written in heaven.

The Bible calls Satan "the prince of the power of the air, the spirit that now worketh in the children of disobedience" (Ephesians 2:2). The wicked one is active, and all his works are destructive. He is a thief, and "the thief cometh not, but for to steal, and to kill, and to destroy" (John 10:10).

Two dangers present themselves to the mind of the believer in Christ. We may either ignore the proximity of the enemy, or we may give him undue attention. Either extreme is wrong. Psalm 23 is not the "enemy Psalm"; it is the "Shepherd Psalm." Yet the enemy's existence is admitted.

We live in a world of enemies. We are forced into combat with them every day. Yet, how tragic that many of God's dear children are furiously fighting foes which they have never even bothered to identify! If you do not know who your enemy is, you can never defeat him. And you might even strike a friend!

It would, of course, be impossible to make an exhaustive list of all enemies which surround God's people. But here are five general categories that nearly include the spectrum of adversaries:

1. *Physical.*

Physical opponents are all around us. But understand this: a physical opponent is not a man who wants to hit you in the jaw! A physical opponent is what you feel after he hits you! Pain, for instance. And sickness.

These bodies of ours have not yet been redeemed. The Bible teaches that we are "waiting for...the redemption of our body" (Romans 8:23). Our souls were redeemed through faith in Christ's work on Calvary. The Holy Spirit, however, is given as "the earnest of our inheritance until the redemption of the purchased possession" (Ephesians 1:14). And "that which is perfect" has not yet come (I Corinthians 13:10).

It is important to recognize that your physical body, which is the temple of the Holy Ghost, can be hurt. It can run a fever. It can break an arm. It can develop cancer. Don't deny it! You can't fight an enemy whose very existence is denied!

Yes, there is healing in the atonement. Jesus Christ does wonderfully and miraculously heal in response to the prayer of faith. But He cannot— note, He *cannot!*—heal the man who refuses to admit that he is sick. Check your New Testament again, observing Jesus' manner of performing miracles. First He would say, "What wilt thou that I

69

shall do unto thee?" (Luke 18:41). The man who will experience the miracle of deliverance cannot deny the reality of physical adversaries.

2. *Mental.*

Inasmuch as the mind is the controlling factor in a man's life, the devil continually connives to dominate his mental faculties. He will tease and torment with suggestions that are so apparently ludicrous that no true child of God will seriously consider them. Then, when the mind is sturdily braced against the lurid and the ridiculous, the wicked one changes his tactics—and he has even been known to quote Scripture!

Frustration, worry, and doubt are very real enemies of the Christian life. Recognize them for what they are. Never suspect that they are friends. You will be forced to combat them as long as you live in this life.

"Be not conformed to this world: but be ye transformed by the renewing of your mind" (Romans 12:2). "Thou wilt keep him in perfect peace, whose mind is stayed on thee" (Isaiah 26:3). You'll never have victory in your life until you have victory in your mind. Know your enemies, and stand against them in Jesus' name.

3. *Moral.*

The devil delights in magnifying man's innate moral weakness. He wastes no time. Waver once in your faith, and strong temptations to immorality will overwhelm you. Don't deny it! To protest the possibility of impropriety is to fall prey to its power.

Israel complained about Moses' long absence at Mt. Sinai. And once they began to find fault, the devil had his foot in the door. So we are not surprised to read that, when Moses and Joshua returned, the people were naked and were in a lewd dance. It'll happen every time.

To boast of your moral strength is to talk foolishly. "In me (that is, in my flesh,) dwelleth no good thing" (Romans 7:18). "Wherefore let him that thinketh he standeth take heed lest he fall" (I Corinthians 10:12). No human being is so advanced spiritually that he is beyond the possibility of this awful sin of lust. Recognize it as an enemy to be dealt with, and do not suppose it to be a dead opponent!

4. *Social.*

It has been well said, "No man is an island." Social isolation is impossible. We are part of a structure called society. Its facets are multiple: there is family, school, club, church, friends, work, town, and nation. The framework is there and we belong to it.

But society—and I do not speak of that "upper crust" thing which fills the society page of the paper, but rather of that glue which binds us one to another—society can be a bitter enemy. Friends will misunderstand you; depend on it. Acquaintances and loved ones alike will try to squeeze you into their mold.

Every relationship which we have with mankind can turn into a frankenstein. Husband-wife, parent-child, employer-employee, buyer-seller, lover-beloved, any or all of these and a thousand other combinations can be a crushing enemy. And they will be, *if* Jesus Christ's claims upon us are usurped by any other.

Examine your life well. Jesus is either Lord of all or He is not Lord at all! His words in Luke 14:26 put it in proper perspective. He said, "If any man come to me, and hate not his father, and mother, and wife, and children, and brethren, and sisters, yea, and his own life also, he cannot be my disciple." Think long and hard on this, sir: those whom you love the most may send your soul to hell!

5. *Spiritual.*

In the final analysis, all enemies are spiritual—for you are spiritual. There is a Godlikeness in every man. And every yearning for the base, the lurid, the mean, the temporal is an attack against your inborn desire for good, for heaven, for God.

The spiritual is the *eternal.* It is *unseen.* It is *known by faith.* These three define our relationship to the spiritual.

Everything that exalts time above eternity is a spiritual enemy. Everything that magnifies the seen above the unseen is a spiritual enemy. Everything which prefers sight to faith is a spiritual enemy.

That philosophy which confines your existence to the period of time between the cradle and the grave is a doctrine of the devil. You were made in God's image. Animal urges will not satisfy your cravings. You know—whether or not you ever read it in the

Bible or heard it from a preacher—you know that you were made for another, and a better, world. Recognize every enemy who perverts that consciousness. This world gives its best first. God saves His best for the world to come.

Yes, we live in a world of enemies. But, "ye are of God, little children, and have overcome them: because greater is he that is in you, than he that is in the world" (I John 4:4). "We are more than conquerors through him that loved us" (Romans 8:37). So we look around and see our enemies, we know they are real and powerful, yet we look to our Good Shepherd and in all confidence say to Him, "Thou preparest a table before me in the presence of mine enemies."

# CELESTIAL CUISINE

Common courtesy says, "Give my compliments to the chef." Good food always calls attention to the one who prepared it, and praise to an accomplished cook is ever in order.

The psalmist saw the bountiful banquet—the celestial cuisine—that is set before the child of God. And he sent his compliments to the "Chef." Recognizing immediately that such profound provision must be a product of Deity, he wrote, "Thou preparest a table before me."

By nature, man is hungry. He is created with cravings—some natural and some transcendent. Think of man only as a time-creature, and he is an animal. Animal urges will satisfy those who are citizens only of time. Give them food, rest, and sex—the three basic animal urges—and they will be content.

But man is a dichotomy: he belongs to time and he belongs to eternity. He has these natural cravings, but he has discovered to his great dismay that a full stomach does not allay every hunger. A whole night's sleep may not secure rest. And nothing, it seems, can long quiet the innate urges toward procreation.

Why? Because we are more than animals. "A man's life consisteth not in the abundance of...things" (Luke 12:15). In another place, the psalmist pictured man's transcendent yearnings like this: "As the hart panteth after the water brooks, so panteth my soul after thee, O God" (Psalm 42:1). Created, as we were, for eternity, we cannot be satisfied with the things of time.

Our Lord was, of course, referring primarily to Himself when He said, "Foxes have holes, and birds of the air have nests; but the Son of man hath not where to lay his head" (Luke 9:58). But that statement also includes every member of Adam's race. Foxes and birds are content with their holes and nests; they are what they have been for millennia. Man, however, always cries out for "a little bit more."

The gospel of Jesus Christ meets man's real needs. Its primary concern is not to fill hungry stomachs but hungry hearts. Knowing that "our earthly house of this tabernacle" must be ultimately "dissolved" (II Corinthians 5:1), *Jesus died to save man's soul, not to fill his pocketbook.*

Let it be firmly established in every mind: earthly blessings are no measure for righteousness. God's gospel promises no gold—not in this life! It deals only with real needs, not temporal ones. We thank our heavenly Father for every material blessing that comes our way, but we never equate blessings with the good news of Bethlehem and Calvary. Material blessings are like vapor; why magnify them out of all proportion?

"Thou preparest a table before me." God's table is filled with good things—things that really satisfy. Men "eat angels' food" (Psalm 78:25)! Mortals assimilate the immortal! Terrestrial tastebuds feast on celestial cuisine! The corruptible dines on the incorruptible!

Mystical? Yes, but very real. God's table is prepared "before me." This is no philosopher's hypothesis, no dreamer's hallucination. It is as palatable as apple pie! You can actually partake of it today! And its benefits are measurable.

Where is this table? How does one go about discovering this gourmet's delight of transcendent nourishment? Is it necessary to be initiated into a secret society of super-spiritual saints before one can sit at such a table full of divine delicacies?

I have good news for you. God's table is just as close as your Bible. Open it and see. Every true hunger of your life can easily be satisfied as soon as you recognize that you belong at this table. Jesus Christ died on Calvary to give you access to its divine provisions.

Every promise in the Book is yours. Some say there are thirty-two thousand promises on the pages of Scripture. Each one of them can be especially meaningful to you.

God's menu is full. There is strength for the weak, courage for the faint, wisdom for the frustrated, happiness for the despondent, contentment for the worried, rest for the weary, healing for the sick, love for the lonely, hope for the discouraged, and life for the dead.

Every genuine need of your life is met in Jesus Christ. He gives light for darkness, joy for sorrow, peace for confusion. He drives away the fear of the future, replacing it with calm assurance.

Beans and potatoes may appease your physical hunger, allowing you to go to bed without gnawing pangs in your stomach. But, mister, beans and potatoes will not prepare you for that moment when you begin to slip into another world. At that hour you need God! And since you don't know when that hour will come, you need God today!

Jesus told about a man who tried to satisfy his soul at earth's table. That man said to his soul, "Soul, thou hast much goods laid up for many years; take thine ease, eat, drink, and be merry. But God said to him, Thou fool, this night thy soul shall be required of thee: then whose shall those things be, which thou hast provided?" (Luke 12:19, 20).

The Bible says, "Meats for the belly, and the belly for meats: but God shall destroy both it and them" (I Corinthians 6:13). Earth's delicacies will do you no good when you step into eternity.

Millions are starving in this world today. The fault, of course, is not theirs; they have no food. And they are dying.

Are you starving? Oh, you may be eating steak every day, yet actually starving to death. God's table is spread before you. Eat, and eat, and eat of it—it is your only hope of everlasting life.

Jesus said, "Labour not for the meat which perisheth, but for that meat which endureth unto everlasting life, which the Son of man shall give unto you" (John 6:27).

"Lord, evermore give us this bread" (John 6:34).

# ANOINTED

"Thou anointest my head with oil." The psalmist is moving into the realm of the sublime. To compare the first part of the twenty-third Psalm with the last part is like comparing the light of sunrise to the brilliance of noontime.

The inspired poet stayed with his shepherd-sheep metaphor as long as he could. Like an airplane, which is designed to soar through the heavens: let it reach a certain speed on the runway and it leaves the ground—so the psalmist takes off! For a while there he was in orbit, but now he has attained escape velocity, and this world has no more hold on him. He is headed straight toward the heart of God.

Did you notice David's change from the third person to the first? He begins by talking *about* God, and concludes by talking *to* Him. Notice the difference. His testimony commences with: "*He* maketh me to lie down...*He* leadeth me...*He* restoreth my soul...*He* leadeth me..." But when he touches on that experience which will transport him to the presence of God, his language changes to "*Thou* art with me...*Thou* preparest a table... *Thou* anointest my head with oil."

His affirmations of God's goodness produced praise. It always does! Start talking *about* the Lord and His concern for you, and you will soon enter the highest realm of communion *with* Him that can be known to mortal man.

The transition has been made. The psalmist has forgotten the illustration of the sheep. He now rapturously worships the Lord, mixing metaphors repeatedly. Who is going to worry about proper syntax when he is in the presence of the Father of lights? At that moment there are often "groanings which cannot be uttered" (Romans 8:26).

"Thou anointest my head with oil." Although the word "anoint" is not part of our common, everyday vernacular, it is used very much in Eastern culture. Basically, there are three types of anointing: *ordinary*, *medical*, and *sacred*. The psalmist, no doubt, had all three in mind.

1. *Ordinary*.

Anointing with scented oils was the final step in a girl's beauty preparations. Ruth was advised to anoint herself before going to meet Boaz (Ruth 3:3). In Proverbs 27:9, ointment is classified with perfumes which "rejoice the heart." Jesus indicated that anointing the head of guests was a mark of hospitality (Luke 7:46). It was discontinued during a time of mourning (II Samuel 14:2). And the dead were prepared for burial by anointing (Mark 14:8; 16:1).

Put it all together: ordinary anointing meant beauty, sweetness, life, and victory over death. This anointing is given to the believer in Jesus every day. He changes ugliness to beauty, making the Bride ever ready to meet her Groom. He gives sweetness and pleasantness for bitterness and malignancy of spirit. He causes us to recognize death as the last enemy to be defeated, then gives hope through His resurrection. The body of the believer who fell asleep is anointed—indicating that the body shall rise again!

Note briefly one other ordinary anointing. Leather shields were anointed with oil to keep them from cracking (Isaiah 21:5)! Keep the anointing, sir, and though the years may produce age, the pliableness and the usefulness of youth will remain. The anointing makes the difference!

2. *Medical.*

Both Isaiah 1:6 and Luke 10:34 indicate that anointing oil was used in the cure of the sick. Our Lord's disciples anointed the sick with oil, "and healed them" (Mark 6:13). Specific instructions are given, in James 5:14, to the elders of the Church. They are to anoint the sick with oil in the name of the Lord. "And the prayer of faith shall save the sick, and the Lord shall raise him up" (James 5:15).

There is healing in the anointing—not in the oil, but in the anointing by faith. God wants you to be well in body.

3. *Sacred.*

The Scriptures abound in sacred anointing. Jacob anointed the stones he had used for a pillow at Bethel. The tabernacle and its furniture were anointed. Prophets, priests, and kings received their divine authority by the anointing oil, symbolic of the Holy Spirit. Such divinely anointed kings were referred to as "the Lord's anointed."

The Hebrew word "Messiah" and the Greek word "Christ" both mean "the anointed One."

Sacred anointing sets that which is anointed aside as belonging in a special way to God. Anointed things and anointed people cannot be desecrated with impunity. The Lord of heaven will interrupt the party of a wicked king who, out of anointed vessels, drinks to his idols! *To be anointed is to belong to God!*

The psalmist wrote, "Thou anointest my head with oil." And we delight in repeating those words today. Because of the daily, divine anointing, we are beautiful and acceptable in His sight. Because of the daily, divine anointing, we have victory over death. Because of the daily, divine anointing, we have healing for our bodies. Because of the daily, divine anointing, we belong to Him!

Thank God, sin's "yoke shall be destroyed because of the anointing"! (Isaiah 10:27).

# WHERE
# THE ANOINTING
# IS NEEDED

All anointing with oil is symbolic. Although God gave specific instructions concerning the preparation and the care of the holy anointing oil in Old Testament scripture (Exodus 30:22-33), there is no indication that the oil itself possessed the inherent power to either bless or to consecrate. The merit was in the obedience.

Anointing with oil is representative of enduement with divine power. Understand: anointing with oil is not an enduement of power—it is *representative* of an enduement of power. The act itself is meaningless, unless done in faith. Thus, anointing is symbolic. The virtue is in the divine unction, not in the olive oil.

Here is an illustration: a woman with an issue of blood came behind Jesus in a crowd, saying to herself, "If I may touch his garment, I shall be whole. But Jesus turned him about, and when he saw her, he said, Daughter, be of good comfort; thy faith hath made thee whole" (Matthew 9:21, 22). It was not her *touch*, it was her *faith* that effected healing.

In like manner, anointing oil may be poured

abundantly on the unbeliever, and it will have no more effect on him than the jostling mob that faithlessly touched Jesus. But let anointing oil contact the head of the man with faith and he will be healed—not by the excellence of the oil but by the trusting recognition of its significance.

Anointing is representative of divine enduement with the power of the Holy Spirit. The Bible says, "God anointed Jesus of Nazareth with the Holy Ghost and with power: who went about doing good, and healing all that were oppressed of the devil; for God was with him" (Acts 10:38). And to His followers Jesus said, "As my Father hath sent me, even so send I you" (John 20:21).

Effective service to our Lord is totally dependent upon divine anointing. Just before His ascension, Jesus commanded His disciples not to begin their ministry immediately but to "wait for the promise of the Father," attesting, "ye shall receive power after that the Holy Ghost is come upon you" (Acts 1:4, 8). Every believer needs that anointing! But where?

The psalmist wrote, "Thou anointest my head with oil" (Psalm 23:5). Three millennia ago the sweet singer of Israel knew where the anointing— the symbol of divine enduement—is needed. *It is needed in the head!*

The New Testament has references to anointing the feet and anointing the eyes, yet neither of these is the fundamental mandate of the victorious Christian life. They only indicate the availability of special anointing for special need.

Man's *mind* needs elevation. It cannot survive in the lowlands of human logic. It must be transformed. "Let this mind be in you, which was also in Christ Jesus" (Philippians 2:5).

Mr. Feeble-mind, in *Pilgrim's Progress*, explained his situation with these words, "My mind is beyond the river that has no bridge." Actually, he wasn't feeble-minded at all, was he? He had discovered the anointing oil which transcends.

Earlier in the twenty-third Psalm the testimony was, "He restoreth my soul." Man's mind was lost by sin, and Jesus' work on Calvary restores it. Regeneration gives back that which was lost.

But now the words are, "Thou anointest my head with oil." This is *more than restoration; it is sublimation!* Restoration resets man in his original upright position, clearing sin's cobwebs from his mind and making him what God originally intended for him to be: a heavenly citizen who lives on planet Earth.

The sublimation of divine anointing, however, goes a step beyond restoration. It lifts restored man to the high and holy position of being an earth creature who is living in heaven!

And the miracle takes place in the mind. This is not to say that the anointed life is a mere mind-over-matter affair. Not at all! It does not deny reality, nor close its eyes to the existence of evil. It simply and wonderfully realizes and admits that unless the mind is transformed the whole life lives in defeat and frustration.

David knew this. On one occasion he sang, "The mountains skipped like rams, and the little hills like lambs" (Psalm 114:4). Do you believe that? I don't! I simply do not believe that mountains ever skipped like rams, or that little hills ever leaped like lambs. "But," some might protest, "the Bible says they did!" No, the Bible only tells us that David *said* they did. You see, the miracle took place within David! His head had been anointed with oil!

Many of God's dear children are falling by the wayside simply because they stop at the point of restoration. Reason says, "Why go further? Why press on for more? You have been lifted out of the pit of sin. Your name is written in heaven. What more could anyone ask?"

Granted, restoration alone equips you for entrance into heaven. But unless you are planning on a trip to glory today, you still have to contend with this world's hills and mountains for a while. And nothing less than divine anointing can gird you for the conflicts on this earth.

The blood of Jesus Christ prepares the heart for eternity. The anointing of the Holy Spirit prepares the mind for time. Both are needed. Their ministries are not identical.

"Have ye received the Holy Ghost since ye believed?" (Acts 19:2).

# "MY CUP RUNNETH OVER"

Service to Jesus must never be equated with defeat. It involves total sacrifice, yes, but to suppose that complete Christian surrender robs the life of abundant happiness and victory is to miss the very essence of this beautiful commitment. As a matter of fact, the only genuinely happy life is the life wholly surrendered to the will of God.

One of the most transcendent expressions about the perpetual rapture of the Christian pilgrim is the psalmist's burst of praise: "My cup runneth over"! Though tested, deprived of earth's dainties, and weary, he sang of an overflowing cup. Though fighting what seemed to be an impossible fight, though backed into a corner from which there seemed to be no escape, though suffering the betrayal of everyone dear to him, the psalmist sang of the immeasurable goodness of God to his soul. He knew, three thousand years ago, that "where sin abounded, grace did much more abound" (Romans 5:20).

Everybody wants to be happy. Even grouches pursue their course of faultfinding because only such nitpicking brings happiness to their perverted minds. We are not morbid by nature. "The pursuit of happiness" is esteemed as one of our inalienable rights.

But sinful man fails in his relentless search for contentment. The taste of the relish wanes. The clover turns brown. The ease becomes wearisome. The honeymoon ends.

Earth's pleasures are measurable. When the game is over, it is over. When the packages are all unwrapped, the lights need to be taken off the Christmas tree—their blinking turns to mockery; it's all over. A new siren must be sought—a dinner table, a New Year's party, Valentine's Day, and on and on and on. Nothing terrestrial has the quality of lasting. There is a deep trough behind every high wave.

As long as sighing dispels rapture, happiness is measurable. It may be real, but it is also minute. It is too little for a creature who was made for eternity. Skeletons, which have the appearance of smiling, aptly depict the hollowness of earth's happiness. How can a man who is to turn to dust be genuinely content?

David's order in the twenty-third Psalm is significant. His triumphant shout, "My cup runneth over," followed his grateful acknowledgment that "Thou anointest my head with oil." Happiness is a state of mind, and true happiness results from the rapture of an anointed mind.

There are three absolute prerequisites to an overflowing cup, and they are all direct results of an anointed mind. They are not natural; they are supernatural. Without them, uninhibited happiness is only a mirage.

*1. First, there must be an honest recognition of personal unworthiness.*

The man who has an inflated idea of his own worth can never be happy. He feels like he deserves more honor than he is getting. And worst of all, he believes that he deserves the honor that he gets—which, of course, causes honor to cease to be honor.

Egoism is the worst foe of happiness. The selfish individual wants everyone to cater to his every whim, and he is not content when they do. He wonders why the delay! He cares nothing for the feelings of others, not realizing that his aloofness is robbing him of the happiness he seeks.

If you want an overflowing cup, learn—in your heart—that you do not deserve even a cup, much less an overflowing one! Recognize each kind word and deed that comes your way as totally undeserved. Don't wear the *mask* of a humble spirit—be genuine!—but know this to be true: if you received what you deserve to receive, you would be in hell today!

If you want an overflowing cup, begin by thanking God for the cup! See the price He paid in order to enrich you, and you will say, "In me, (that is, in my flesh,) dwelleth no good thing" (Romans 7:18).

2. *Second, there must be a true recognition of limitations.*

You are not responsible for the attitudes and the actions of others. You are responsible only for your own attitudes and actions.

Simply put, this frees a man from the power of circumstances. Paul could sing in prison because God never assigned to him the liability for a Philippian magistrate's actions. If Paul lived right, no Grecian dungeon could steal his song.

This world is full of things over which you have no control. So don't let them keep you from happiness! Refuse to live "under" the circumstances; live above them! If a man hates you for doing right, that's his problem, not yours.

Oh, circumstances will, of course, send the dedicated child of God to his knees—but not in quest of happiness! He will pray and work and give in order to improve external conditions. His recognition of personal limitations will, however, deprive this planet of its power to pirate his peace. Whatever may happen all around him, his cup overflows!

3. *Third, there must be a genuine recognition of priorities.*

What is happiness? Is it money in the bank or peace in the heart? Is it a healthy body or a healthy soul? Is it praise from men or praise from God?

The happy man—the man with an overflowing cup—is the one whose eyes are open to see the difference between time and eternity, between the seen and the unseen, between the important and the unimportant. Time cannot hurt him; he is a citizen of eternity. He knows that if his "earthly house of this tabernacle were dissolved," he has "a building of God, an house not made with hands, eternal in the heavens" (II Corinthians 5:1). You may bring tears to his eyes, pain to his body, and discord to his life; but he has higher priorities than any of these things. And his happiness remains.

The happy man knows that "these things shall be dissolved," so his sight is set on "new heavens and a new earth, wherein dwelleth righteousness" (II Peter 3:11, 13). He is sublimated. And his cup overflows. If he were living for this world, discouragement would overwhelm him. But he is living for another world, and time cannot touch him.

Do you want to be happy? Let it begin in your head. Seek divine anointing. Let God set your perspective straight. He will let you see your own unworthiness, He will show you your limitations, and He will help set your priorities in order. The light will come. You may still be in this planet's prison, but all who are near will hear your "Hallelujah! My cup is running over!"

# "GOODNESS, YOU'RE FOLLOWING ME!"

The follower is being followed! The man who can honestly say about Jesus, "He leadeth me," can go on to shout, "Surely goodness and mercy shall follow me all the days of my life."

The emphatic word "surely" leaves no room for doubt. The matter has been settled once and for all. The trial was complete and fair. The jury has been sent home. All further discussion is wasted time and effort. We leave hypotheses to others; this is the most certain truth in all creation: if I follow God, goodness and mercy will follow me!

Goodness follows the believer. Let us be careful, however, in our understanding of terms. A casual glance at the psalmist's expression might cause some to suppose that the promise is to make the believer good. But read it again: "Surely goodness...shall *follow* me."

It is true, of course, that the righteousness of Christ is imputed to the believer. We stand "justified freely by his grace" (Romans 3:24). But understand: faith in Jesus' blood does not make *us* good; it is a miracle of the unmerited goodness of Christ being imputed *to* us. As long as we live in these earthly tabernacles, we will have to confess "that in me (that is, in my flesh,) dwelleth no good thing" (Romans 7:18).

The psalmist was not discussing *becoming* good; he was rejoicing in being *followed* by goodness. As a man, he would still have limitations, he would still be weak, he would still make mistakes. But as he looked behind him, he saw the goodness of God. The Lord was fitting the pieces together, vetoing human inadequacies, bringing good out of difficulties.

You see, we are poor judges of goodness. We want to do good for our children, so we spare them the struggles we went through. And we aren't good to them at all! We rob them of the tests that make them strong!

Somehow, we have foolishly equated goodness with pleasure. But that kind of logic supposes that lollypops and candy bars are better for you than peas and carrots! How foolish! The child is no judge of what is good for him. His parents must make the decisions. Leave the kid alone and he will stay up all night, skip school, live in front of a television set, and eat little more than candy, cokes, and hamburgers. And the reason is apparent: he simply does not yet know what is good for him.

In like manner we, as God's children, cannot now know what is good for us. We are in no position to make decisions; all the facts have not been given to us. So what are we to do? I'm so glad you asked! We are to follow Jesus! That's all? That's all!

When I lay out my own course, I detour around all storms. I select the easiest work with the most pay. I endeavor to avoid anything that would cause pain, discomfort, or tears. I elect always to have the companionship of the most congenial friends. I avoid any war.

But when I follow the Lord, He leads me in the most unpleasant places—because He knows what is good for me. "When he hath tried me, I shall come forth as gold" (Job 23:10).

Let it be clearly understood—and this truth is vital to daily victory—that these things, these tests, which come to the Christian are not good! But they are good *for* us, for goodness is following us! Our heavenly Father has higher goals for us than the mere euphoria of the moment. And He makes even the wrath of man to praise Him (Psalm 76:10).

In another place the psalmist confided, "It is good for me that I have been afflicted; that I might learn thy statutes" (Psalm 119:71). There are lessons which cannot be learned in a dress parade. Only the firing line puts the mettle in the soldier.

It was good for Abraham to lay his only son on the altar of sacrifice. It was good for Moses to tend sheep in a desert for forty years. It was good for David to fight lions and bears. It was good for Paul to spend years of suffering in cruel prisons. It was good for John to be exiled to Patmos.

The entire Bible is replete with accounts of men and women of faith who endured the severest tests known to man. And in each case it was not the test but the goodness that followed it which proved a transcendent blessing. For example, many men went to prison, but not many preached from prison as Paul did. Goodness followed him.

"But," we complain, "I don't see how any good can come out of *my* situation! Goodness isn't following me now!"

Then we are right! As long as we look at the difficulty, as long as we try to analyze the merits of the test, no good can come out of it. None at all. When our eyes are on the problem, the miracle of divine grace is defeated. We are to look "unto Jesus the author and finisher of our faith" (Hebrews 12:2).

Keith Creighton, my assistant pastor and a devout student of Greek, has a beautiful translation of Romans 8:28. It goes like this: "We know that God works through all things for the good of those who love Him and who are called according to His purpose."

The promise has been woefully misunderstood. We have been led to believe that only "good" things happen to the believer—and we buoy up our positivity by singing gustily, "Something good is going to happen to you this very day!" And our twisted thinking conjures pictures of money, fortune, laughter, health.

But read it again. The promise is not that only "good" things will happen to the believer; it is that God works through all things for the good of the believer. He will not replace the storm, but He will walk with you on top of the waters. He will not deliver John from Patmos, but will transform that Alcatraz into a place of revelation of the King of kings and Lord of lords. Mister, when you see the heavens opened, you forget Patmos!

Every day of my life brings a new attack from the wicked one. But because I am following the Lord, goodness is following me. The things that were to have occasioned my downfall have made me stronger in Christ. "The trials make me stronger than I have been before."

Yes, difficulties are part and parcel of the Christian life. They always have been, and until we leave this world they always will be. But goodness is following the follower of the Lord, picking up the pieces, defeating the devil, and turning testing to triumph.

This is the life of faith. I don't have to watch in all directions. If I keep my eyes on Jesus, His goodness will take care of all around me. "Surely goodness . . . shall follow me all the days of my life; and I will dwell in the house of the Lord for ever."

# MERCY

Every conscientious Christian has cause for concern when he considers the collage of flotsam and jetsam in the wake of his voyage through life. Attempts toward perfection are very often woefully defeated. Blunders abound. Vows are made—and broken.

We aspire to leave an uncluttered trail, so others may clearly see the way and follow us to heaven. But the honest recollection of our chronic mistakes and falterings causes us to wonder why the great God of heaven should tolerate us any longer! We recall the ideals and the aspirations which filled our mind at the outset of our Christian journey, and we compare them with the tragic way we have fallen short. And we despair even of living. Why should we clutter up the earth any longer?! We grovel in the muck and mire of our own flaws.

Then—at a time when we least expect it—we are shocked by a word of appreciation. A letter from a friend reads something like this: "I just wanted to let you know what an inspiration your life has been to me. I've been watching you, and have been impressed by your faithfulness to God in times of severe pressures. Many would have fallen by the wayside, but you remained strong. You never wavered in your consecration to the right, but stood tall and true against every attack of the wicked one."

The letter goes on: "I'm not a person who finds it easy to express himself. Many times I've wanted to simply take your hand and say, 'Thank for being such a shining example of the power and courage which God gives, and for the personal help your dedication has been to me,' but when I stood before you, words failed me. I muttered a clumsy greeting and hurried away. You must have thought me crude or unfriendly; but the truth is, I feel so inadequate in the presence of a saint like you. And that's why I'm trying to express my feelings of gratitude in this letter."

*We can hardly believe our eyes. Hurriedly we check to see if we're reading someone else's mail. But, no, it's addressed to us. Tears start down our cheeks as we continue reading:* "There's a special reason why I'm writing at this time. The past few weeks have been the most trying time of my life. I have stood frustrated on the very brink of despair. All life's bubbles, for me, had burst. Every dream had irrevocably disappeared. My heart was crushed so much that I thought I would die. I tried to pray, but I confess to you that I thought God had left me. Serious questions about His goodness, and even of His existence, preyed on my mind.

"I finally came to a place where I never thought I

would be—I wanted to die. And suicide seemed to be the only way. 'Why live? Why go on like this? Why keep on trying? Why not get out of this farce called life? There's no existence after death, no heaven, no hell, no God—or He would have answered my prayers.' These kinds of thoughts invaded me from all sides. And I actually made plans to end it all.

"Then I remembered you. My trials are nothing to compare with what you've been through. And you never lost faith! You kept a smile on your face and a song in your heart through the time of crushing. I remembered how you displayed unshakable strength when the devil hit you the hardest. I saw you crying at the altar several times and I knew you were like Jesus in the garden of Gethsemane—you were fighting hell, and winning!"

*Fresh tears are now mingling with obviously dried ones on the last page of the letter, which continues:* "I owe my life to you and your dedication to God. How can I thank you!? Like so many others in our church who have watched you through the years, I have admired the way you have allowed the Spirit of Jesus to shine through you. Maybe someday, in the world to come, I can adequately tell you what a blessing you have been to me. But this I know: your example of the power of a consecrated life to God is the reason I'm not in hell today."

We cannot stand. We fall down into a chair and bow our head to our knees. We cry, "Lord, a moment ago I was thinking of what a mess I've made of my life. You know, Lord, that I was being honest: I *have* miserably failed You. I have stumbled, staggered, wavered. I have made more than my share of mistakes. And those times at the altar—You know, Lord, *I was feeling sorry for myself!* It was not a mock humility that made me talk of my weakness—I *am* weak. I know my own heart, and I have been the poorest of examples. How could the writer of this letter see any good in me?"

We open the Bible. The answer must be in the Word. We begin to read: "Surely goodness and mercy shall follow me." There's the answer! Mercy is following me! Divine goodness is there, turning tragedies into blessings. And divine mercy also follows me, displaying the grace of God—turning darkness to light.

My friend looked at me, and he saw the mercy of God! He never saw my errors. He never saw the falterings of my faith. He never saw the weakness of my soul. He saw the mercy of God! It's a miracle!

Like a mother who follows her child through the house—picking up after him, putting things back in order again—so the goodness and mercy of God follow the believer! *God's goodness is His blessing, and God's mercy is His forgiveness.* These clear the trail behind us, so others won't stumble over either our trials or our blunders. They will see the grace of God!

"There is therefore now no condemnation to them which are in Christ Jesus, who walk not after the flesh, but after the Spirit" (Romans 8:1). Of course there is no condemnation! How can there be? Because I follow Jesus, His mercy follows me!

# ALL
# THE DAYS
## OF MY LIFE

The psalmist has now outgrown his years of childhood and adolescence. He has long since passed the paltry plateau of pining for pleasure and prosperity on this planet. His vision has been enlarged, his perspective has been lifted, his horizon has been sublimated. Questions of relevance have faded. David has discovered what life is all about—and he rejoices!

The song has reached its crescendo. All music now reads "*fortissimo*"—very loud. Subtle moods are over. Every instrument is playing. All "stops" are out. The tune that began with testings will end in triumph.

You can't feel blue when you sing this song: "Surely goodness and mercy shall follow me all the days of my life: and I will dwell in the house of the Lord for ever"! Gloom flies from such a testimony about the faithfulness of God. This present world loses its appeal—for it is seen as it truly is.

It would be difficult indeed to find a phrase anywhere in literature which could equal the comprehensiveness of these syllables of the psalmist:

"All the days of my life." Four profound truths here present themselves to the mind of the believer:

1. *"Life."*

Life is a miracle. It is a gift from heaven. In the garden of Eden, "the Lord God formed man of the dust of the ground, and breathed into his nostrils the breath of life; and man became a living soul" (Genesis 2:7). Life is God-breathed.

To assume that life is a mere product of the combination of the genes of a man and a woman is to miss the truth altogether. Life is a miracle. Scientists may frantically search in their quest to discover the mystery of life, but their test tubes will never reveal the answer. The creation of life is in God's hands alone.

It is important to recognize and believe this. For until man accepts the absolute authority of God over life, he will continually seek to circumvent the divine plan. "And he is before all things, and by him all things consist" (Colossians 1:17). God not only gives all life, He sustains all life.

2. *"My life."*

David knew that life is both a miracle and a gift. God gives life to men. (Understand: we are not, at this point, discussing life after death. The subject in this phrase is life on this earth.)

God gave life to you. Maybe you didn't want it, but He gave it to you anyhow. This miracle of life is yours. You may, if you wish, destroy it—but you cannot reverse it. Before you take any drastic action, however, you had better discover the purpose for your life. Since God created it, He is the only One who can provide the answers.

"My life." I have been entrusted with a miracle. God did not make a mistake when He created me. If I consider life a failure, it is because I have made it so. I was given exactly what every son of Adam has been given—life. My circumstances may be different than others, but if I suppose that mere circumstances make life meaningful, I need to examine myself and others much more carefully.

It's your life. Nobody is responsible for it but you. And you are not accountable for the lives of others. "So then every one of us shall give account of himself to God" (Romans 14:12).

3. *The days of my life.*

Life is not a mystical nonentity. It is a sequence of small periods of time—days, for example. And those little segments make up the entirety of your existence on earth.

It is foolish to attempt to judge your life by looking at the total number of years you celebrate on your birthday. That is yesterday. And you don't live in yesterday. It would be equally ridiculous to judge life by the possibility of what may happen tomorrow. You don't live in tomorrow.

You live today—that's all. Life is not the blunders of the past or the propects of the future. Life is now. Today. Quit this business of looking at something that does not exist. What are you doing with *this* moment? That's the question.

Life is days, hours, minutes. And each one of

them is important. When we stand before God our "life" will not be examined; our "days" will be!

"But my life is a failure," someone says. What do you mean by that? Is this moment a failure? That's what your life is, you know! Then make the next moment meaningful, and you will be on the road to victory.

4. *"All the days of my life."*

This is the promise of God: "I will never leave thee, nor forsake thee" (Hebrews 13:5). When will He be with me? All my life? No, that's too nebulous. He will be with me "all the *days* of my life."

God is interested in my days! The little things which make up my existence are important to Him! Every day has the promise of the divine presence! Every morning brings the assurance of being followed by His goodness and mercy!

I need a promise like that! Otherwise I might suspect, once in a while, that God has forgotten me. When a day comes along in which nothing seems to "go right," I am tempted to suppose that the Lord has other things to do—and that I'm going to have to simply endure this rotation of the earth and hope for a brighter tomorrow.

No! A thousand times, no! There is no tomorrow! "This is the day which the Lord hath made; we will rejoice and be glad in it" (Psalm 118:24). I will rejoice today! In this circumstance! For He is with me! Now!

"Surely"—no question about it—"goodness and mercy shall follow me all the days of my life." God's

105

calendar is full. *He has made an appointment to be with me all day every day;* and He keeps His appointments!

This is not merely "the power of positive thinking"; it is the promise of the living God. He is with you on Monday as well as Sunday. Reach out in faith, and you will feel His presence right now!

# "MY LIFE"

When the psalmist wrote, "Surely goodness and mercy shall follow me all the days of my life" his view was both behind and before him. "God will be with me because He has been with me." The Lord's faithfulness in days gone by assures His faithfulness in the days to come. "Jesus Christ the same yesterday, and today, and forever" (Hebrews 13:8). What He has been, He will be.

David remembered his life. And from his perspective, the scene was not always beautiful. He had failed God more than once. He had strayed from the path of righteousness. Willfully he had done wrong. Intentionally he had disobeyed the divine directive. In his heart he knew that the blame was all his own.

If these lines were written toward the end of David's days on earth, he had an awful diary to review. He had written an autobiography that included lust, immorality, murder, and fraud. He had caused one of his sons to slay another of his sons. He had precipitated the events which caused another son to die in ignominy, hanging by his hair in a tree and having an arrow shot through his heart by David's own general; and David's pitiful cry, "O my son Absalom, my son, my son Absalom! would God I had died for the, O Absalom, my son, my son!" (II Samuel 18:33) did not bring his son back to life again. He had also turned the scale which caused his best friend and counselor to commit suicide.

The list goes on and on and on. And the sweet singer of Israel must have remembered his mistakes when he wrote the twenty-third Psalm.

We must clearly understand, however, that David did not simply walk through life, leaving a trail of blood and regrets. He was, in fact, a man after God's own heart. When he sinned, he humbled himself and confessed his wrong. There were more victories than defeats in his life—but tragically, it is easier for most of us to remember a man's mistakes than to recount his times of faithfulness.

But whatever lay behind him, when David wrote the words "my life" he had cause to rejoice in the grace of God which triumphs over human weakness. The psalmist did not seek out the debris of the past, using his faults as an excuse for surrender to the flesh. He saw how God had not only cleaned up the debris but had made something good and beautiful out of David's life. Goodness and mercy had followed him.

So when the psalmist wrote of his "life" he could write with confidence. He refused to be haunted by skeletons in the closet of his past. Victoriously he could sing, "Because thou hast been my help, therefore in the shadow of thy wings will I trust" (Psalm 63:7).

Yes, there had been a Bathsheba in David's life, but there had also been a Goliath. The immorality had been wrong; the victory for the God of Israel had been right—but that doesn't tell the whole story: The psalmist humbly sought the Lord for forgiveness. God heard his petition, and to David and Bathsheba was born a son named Solomon, who built the first great Temple, wrote the Proverbs, and, except for Jesus Christ, was the wisest man who ever lived! Once again, a man's faith in God turned tragedy into triumph.

None of this, however, should lead us to suppose that David ever presumed upon the grace of God. The mere fact that the Lord had intervened so many times—overriding the psalmist's blunderings, and turning them into actual blessings—never, never, never led David into the nonchalant philosophy of: "So what? It doesn't matter whether I do right or wrong; God will fix it up for me!"

No! David learned—oh! how he learned!—that "whatsoever a man soweth, that shall he also reap" (Galatians 5:7). He paid dearly for every time he stepped out of line. Although God wrought victory out of defeat, the psalmist never—in this life—got over the personal pang of failure. His tears were real.

I am writing these thoughts very late at night in the Baptist Memorial Hospital in Kansas City,

Missouri. It is Friday. Three days ago I went into surgery for the removal of two more cancers. God was very good; the malignancies were isolated; and much to the surprise of many, tomorrow I go home!

Tuesday morning, lying for one hour in the quietness of the "surgery holding" room, I thought about "my life." What is it? To the people around me, I'm just a name on a list. They roll my bed around as it suits them. Soon my turn will come and they'll roll me into surgery—then this group can draw a line through my name. They've done their duty.

Somewhere in this hospital, I thought, in some of the records they have on me, there's a little space yet to be checked. I don't know what name they have on it—probably "deceased." And someday, in this hospital or some other, if Jesus tarries, a mark will be made in that little square. I will have checked out of the hospital without going through the front office.

Morbid? No, I wasn't being morbid. I fully expected to come through the operation. But I was just thinking, as did David, of this thing which I call "my life." A successful operation does not tell the story. A check in a square does not tell the story. A line drawn through my name does not tell the story.

This thing which I call "my life" is the most important thing I've got. Others may turn the page and forget it, but I can't. Oh yes, it is as crowded with regrets as was David's. Hot tears stream down my face when I think of my failures. The debris of

110

my past has been disgusting to me, and it crucified God's Son.

But God has been good! He has cleared up the mess. In spite of my weakness, my humanness, my sinfulness, He has used me. And I marvel that He could make anything useful out of such obstinate clay.

My life is not over. It never will be. Let cancer destroy every fiber and every bone in my body, let this tabernacle be returned to dust, I will continue to live—somewhere. And where I will be in that world to come is being determined by what I do with "my life" today. If I can honestly say, "The Lord is my shepherd," I can also confidently affirm that "Surely goodness and mercy shall follow me all the days of my life." Then, with calm assurance, I can know that "I will dwell in the house of the Lord forever."

James wrote, "For what is your life? It is even a vapour, that appeareth for a little time, and then vanisheth away" (4:14).

Moses also wrote, "In the morning it flourisheth, and groweth up; in the evening it is cut down, and withereth. . . . We spend our years as a tale that is told. The days of our years are threescore years and ten; and if by reason of strength they be fourscore years, yet is their strength labour and sorrow; for it is soon cut off, and we fly away" (Psalm 90:6, 9, 10). Yes, we fly away, but where?

Our Lord looked at life, and asked, "For what is a

man advantaged, if he gain the whole world, and lose himself, or be cast away?" (Luke 9:25).

After the operation the doctor told me I have a new lease on life. He was referring of course, to my days on this planet. Only Jesus can give a lease on eternal life. He cares so much for your life that He gave His. Do you care where you will spend eternity? Someday you will care; but if you reject Jesus today, your concern in the world to come will be too late.

# PUTTING IT
## ALL
### TOGETHER

"And I shall dwell in the house of the Lord for ever." The twenty-third Psalm is a Jacob's ladder; it may be set up on earth, but it reaches into heaven. It may speak of pastures, rivers, valleys, fears, rods, staffs, enemies, anointings, and cups, but it cannot close with such discussions.

Without this last phrase, the entire psalm would be a meaningless facade. Every line, every phrase, every idea would be a joke. All relevance would disappear. The beauty would fade. For, you see, even faith and love cannot abide without hope!

The Christian life is, here and now, a wonderful life. It is, in fact, the only answer to man's innate quest for happiness. It abounds in victory, in rejoicing, and in love. Human philosophies fail to provide even one good substitute for the transcendent Christian life.

Of course there are tests. To say that the Christian life is a wonderful life must not be interpreted to mean that it is always full of sunshine, roses, and sunny days. Battles are as regular as the turn of the clock. Physical, mental, moral, and spiritual enemies conspire to take their toll on the true

113

believer in Christ. Yet, in spite of this, every real Christian would not trade his experiences for all the wealth of the world. He has found true happiness.

Some have become so excited about the daily victories in the life of faith that they have foolishly testified that they enjoy this new life in Christ so much they would be Christians even though there were no life to come! The intent is to be commended, but the understanding of the facts leaves much to be desired.

The truth is this: *if there were no life to come, neither you nor I would live for God, no matter how much we may now declare that we enjoy the Christian life!* Only our confidence in the reality of eternity effects joy and happiness today! Destroy our belief in the resurrection and in the glories of heaven, and every incentive to day-by-day victory for Jesus would be gone!

Who enjoys suffering? Who enjoys constant pressure from the wicked one? Who enjoys sacrifice? Who enjoys self-denial? Who enjoys a broken heart? Who enjoys carrying a heavy load? Who enjoys agonizing in prayer over souls lost in sin? Who enjoys tribulation, persecution, misunderstandings, confrontations with the flesh—even though they be for Christ's sake?

The apparent answer is, "Nobody! Nobody actually *enjoys* such adversities. Christians may learn to endure them, but it is impossible to delight in them." That is the apparent answer, but it is wrong. The fact is, God's children genuinely "glory" in "infirmities." They "take pleasure in infirmities, in reproaches, in necessities, in persecutions, in distresses for Christ's sake" (II Corinthians 12:9, 10).

Why? Because they love pain? No! They "reckon that the sufferings of this present time are not worthy to be compared with the glory which shall be revealed in us" (Romans 8:18). The saints testify, "Though our outward man perish, yet the inward man is renewed day by day. For our light affliction, which is but for a moment, worketh for us a far more exceeding and eternal weight of glory" (II Corinthians 4:16, 17).

Still some would insist that the Christian life is best, whether or not there is an eternity, because it is the only life with peace and joy. But what produces the peace and joy? The assurance that there is a better life to come! Take that away, and you take away your peace and joy.

Paul said it as clearly as it can be said, "If in this life only we have hope in Christ, we are of all men most miserable" (I Corinthians 15:19). The basic "stuff" which makes Christianity what it is is the hope we have in the world to come. Hope is the glue which holds every facet of this wonderful life together.

Read the first seven verses of Ephesians, Chapter Two. The whole purpose of the miracle of salvation is "that in the ages to come he might show the exceeding riches of his grace in his kindness toward us through Jesus Christ" (Ephesians 2:7). There is no way to divorce hope from the Christian life.

David was aware of this. He could not leave us in

forced prostration in green pastures, or seeing ourselves in still waters, or walking in right paths, or being comforted by the divine protection, or reveling in the presence of enemies, or being anointed with oil, or rejoicing over circumstances. He could not even leave us being led through the valley of the shadow of death; he must tell us what's beyond that valley! Nor could he leave us with the mere confidence that goodness and mercy are following us; these are behind us, and we are marching ahead. All these truths are good, but they are not enough.

So the psalmist puts it all together. He puts meaning into every phrase of his song when he shouts, "And I shall dwell in the house of the Lord for ever!"

Now it makes sense! The pressures of this life are robbed of their power to hurt. The vision of the believer is lifted. He sees another world, and that rapturous vista so triumphantly transcends the swamps of this planet that he shouts with Job:

"Oh that my words were now written! oh that they were printed in a book! That they were graven with an iron pen and lead in the rock for ever. For I know that my redeemer liveth, and that he shall stand at the latter day upon the earth: And though after my skin worms destroy this body, yet in my flesh shall I see God: Whom I shall see for myself, and mine eyes shall behold, and not another" (Job 19:23-27).

The devil can't touch a hope like that!

# PERIOD

Only one punctuation mark can properly close the twenty-third Psalm—a period. The whole story has been told, and there are to be no "repeats" in the ages to come—no more need of a Shepherd, no more discipline because of waywardness, no more ugly self-revelations, no more possibility of walking in wrong paths, no more valley of the shadow of death, no more rod and staff, no more enemies, no more need for anointing, no more need for goodness and mercy to follow us.

When the psalmist said, "And I shall dwell in the house of the Lord for ever," he closed with a period. The little word "dwell" tells it all. There will be experiences by the billions, yes; but the time of probation will be forever over.

The step from this world to the next one is a period, not a comma. Oh, life will continue, but it will not change courses. The last page of your Bible explains it graphically: "He that is unjust, let him be unjust still: and he which is filthy, let him be filthy still: and he that is righteous, let him be righteous still: and he that is holy let him be holy still" (Revelation 22:11).

There's no change beyond the period. Other things may be written, but they cannot change what was written before the period. A comma, for instance, allows for a total about-face. A semicolon allows a complete qualifying clause. A colon allows a dependent clause or phrase. But once you put down a period, that sentence is over.

We are all racing toward the final punctuation, and it will be a period. We will step into another, and eternal, world. There will be no reincarnation, no "second chance" after death, no use of the eraser in total annihilation. We will be forced to say with Pilate, "What I have written, I have written" (John 19:22)—period.

The period at the end of the sentence is what makes life so important. Once it's over, it's over. And we have no idea when we will be forced to make a period and put down the pencil forever. That's why it's so vital to keep our experience with God up to date.

Many, many people have to put the periods in the wrong place. They never finish the thesis. They never put it all together. They never come to the place they can confidently say, "I shall dwell in the house of the Lord for ever." And, mister, until you can say that, you are not ready to put the period on your life!

But how can a man have such confidence? How can he say with assurance that he is ready to put the period on his life—to step into the world to come?

Simon Peter had the answer. He said to Jesus, "Lord, to whom shall we go? thou hast the words of eternal life" (John 6:68). He had heard the message of John the Baptist, "He that believeth on the Son hath everlasting life: and he that believeth not the Son shall not see life; but the wrath of God abideth on him" (John 3:36). And he had heard Jesus Himself say, "Except a man be born again, he cannot see the kingdom of God" (John 3:3).

The apostle Paul, who had preached justification by faith in the blood of Jesus, had the answer. Facing execution, he could say, "I am now ready to be offered, and the time of my departure is at hand. I have fought a good fight, I have finished my course, I have kept the faith: Henceforth there is laid up for me a crown of righteousness, which the Lord, the righteous judge, shall give me at that day: and not to me only, but unto all them also that love his appearing" (II Timothy 4:6-8).

When the final period is written on your life, you will continue to exist. But you will have made your final choice between heaven and hell, between eternal life and eternal death. All change must be this side of the period, this side of the grave.

The twenty-third Psalm is beautiful. It tells of God's faithful dealings with His children. It pictures His love and His long-suffering. It displays His strength when we are weak, His companionship when we are lonely, His joy when we are sad.

But the twenty-third Psalm, like life, must come

to an end. It must have its final punctuation mark, and for the sweet singer of Israel it was a mark of rapture. His final "period" was a move to the presence of God forever.

Where will *you* be when you put the period on your days on earth?